19212

D1118941

Who Do You Think You Are?

Digging for Your Family Roots

Who Do You Think You Are?

Digging for Your Family Roots

by SUZANNE HILTON

THE WESTMINSTER PRESS
PHILADELPHIA

BOOK DESIGN BY DOROTHY E. JONES

PUBLISHED BY THE WESTMINSTER PRESS®
PHILADELPHIA, PENNSYLVANIA

PRINTED IN THE UNITED STATES OF AMERICA

Library of Congress Cataloging in Publication Data

Hilton, Suzanne.
  Who do you think you are?

  Bibliography: p.
  Includes index.
  SUMMARY: Step-by-step instructions on how to trace one's ancestors and construct a family tree.
    1. Genealogy—Juvenile literature.
2. United States—Genealogy—Juvenile literature.
[1. Genealogy] I. Title.
CS16.H54   929'.1   75-40274
ISBN 0-664-32587-4

CONTENTS

WARNING:
This Book Could
Be Habit-forming!

Just the way you can get devoted to reading mystery stories, you can get hooked on digging for your own roots.

You may not turn into a family history addict today, but someday you may find yourself in a city far from home searching for someone you never knew who has been dead 250 years! You will be breathing the same air he breathed and marveling at the same mountain or prairie view that once turned him on. And because he is in your blood, you will understand how he felt.

Do you ever wonder who you are? You are a social security number where you work and another number to an insurance company, to the hospital where you had your tonsils out, and on your driver's license. At school you are a locker number, a library card number, and even a number showing where you stand in the class. In sports, your shirt has a number on the back. Even the school itself is a number that you listen for on the radio when the weather is bad. Whatever happened to *people?*

Do you ever wonder what makes you *you* and different from your best friend? Do you love to be outdoors in the rain while some of your friends stay inside, making up excuses for not coming out until the weather clears up? Perhaps it's because of your ancestors. Some people came from such dry country that rain was a real reason to celebrate and your ancestors lifted their faces into the welcome rain joyfully—just the way you feel now. Perhaps you are a boy who has felt the urge to stand up and dance all alone just as your ancestors did in the old country—but a man dancing all alone seems unmanly in this country.

Today young people all across North America are wanting to find out more about their missing ancestors, whose genes are still alive in their own bodies. If you are black, you may be glad your ancestors gave you hair that makes up nicely into an Afro. If you have good teeth, you may be thankful when your father says, "All my family had good teeth." One ancestor may have given you your short, stubby figure and another your gift in mathematics. You might enjoy getting to know them.

No one ancestor is responsible for you. That is what makes the hunting so much fun. Only a small bit of each one has gone into making you the very special person you are.

This book tells you how to unbury those people. Your story will be entirely different from your best friend's story. You will be surprised, often delighted, with each new discovery, and never bored. How could you be? It's all about *you!*

HAPPY HUNTING

8 My g. grandfather
Born:
Where:
Died:
Where:

9 My g. grandmother
Born:
Where:
Died:
Where:

10 My g. grandfather
Born:
Where:
Died:
Where:

11 My g. grandmother
Born:
Where:
Died:
Where:

12 My g. grandfather
Born:
Where:
Died:
Where:

13 My g. grandmother
Born:
Where:
Died:
Where:

14 My g. grandfather
Born:
Where:
Died:
Where:

15 My g. grandmother
Born:
Where:
Died:
Where:

4 My grandfather
Born:
Where:
Died:
Where:

5 My grandmother
Born:
Where:
Died:
Where:

6 My grandfather
Born:
Where:
Died:
Where:

7 My grandmother
Born:
Where:
Died:
Where:

2 My father
Born:
Where:
Died:
Where:

3 My mother
Born:
Where:
Died:
Where:

1 My name
Born:
Where:
Died:
Where:

1

Going Ahead — Backwards

Back in the old days—at least thirty years ago—many people searched for their ancestors for snobbish reasons. The results were frustrating. Either they discovered that their ancestors were mostly the hardworking farmers who turned this land into a nation or else they found ancestors who looked so great that the searchers themselves felt like potatoes in comparison—their best parts buried underground.

Today's ancestor hunter is not looking for fame or fortune. He is looking for himself. And he does it by starting with what he knows right now and moving backwards slowly into the past.

What do you know about yourself now? Your name and birthday. Draw a chart like the one in the illustration and put your name on the line after #1. Write your birthday—and all the other dates you write from now on—without punctuation, like this: 3 Sep 1960.

Add your parents' names. Your father will be #2, because a father's number on the chart is always double the number in front of his child's name.

Your mother is #3. Be sure to write her maiden name—that is, the name she was given at birth and used before she married your father. Ask both your parents for their exact birth dates (and stifle that impulse to say "Wow!" after the year) and where they were born. Then write down when and where they were married. Already you have completed the second generation.

The family tree has begun to branch. Finding all the names and dates of grandparents is harder. Be sure to write their complete names, including middle names if you can learn them. "Grandma Smith" will not do. Write the name she used before she married and even thought of being a grandmother, so that her family line can be followed too. Your paternal grandfather will have a number double that of your father. Your maternal grandfather's number will be twice that of his daughter. You have already gone back fifty years or more.

There are eight great-grandparents to find. You have a clue to the last names of the men because you have the last name of each of their children. But their wives will add four new names to the list and each of those will start another branch of the family tree.

You are probably looking at some empty lines by now. Every one of them represents a real person—someone who once lived, fell in love, married, and had children. And because they did, you are here. Their blood runs through your veins. You can't just leave their places empty. So how do you find people who have been missing a hundred years or more?

The most important single thing you will do in

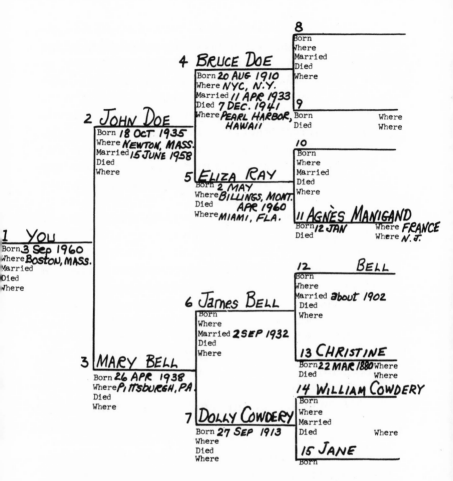

8
Born
Where
Married
Died
Where

4 BRUCE DOE
Born **20 AUG 1910**
Where **NYC, N.Y.**
Married **11 APR 1933**
Died **7 DEC. 1941**
Where **PEARL HARBOR,
HAWAII**

9
Born   Where
Died   Where

2 JOHN DOE
Born **18 OCT 1935**
Where **NEWTON, MASS.**
Married **15 JUNE 1958**
Died
Where

10
Born
Where
Married
Died
Where

5 ELIZA RAY
Born **2 MAY**
Where **BILLINGS, MONT.**
Died **APR 1960**
Where **MIAMI, FLA.**

11 AGNÈS MANIGAND
Born **12 JAN**   Where **FRANCE**
Died   Where **N. J.**

1 YOU
Born **3 Sep 1960**
Where **Boston, MASS.**
Married
Died
Where

12   BELL
Born
Where
Married **about 1902**
Died
Where

6 James BELL
Born
Where
Married **2 SEP 1932**
Died
Where

13 CHRISTINE
Born **22 MAR 1880** Where
Died   Where

3 MARY BELL
Born **26 APR 1938**
Where **PITTSBURGH, PA.**
Died
Where

14 WILLIAM COWDERY
Born
Where
Married
Died   Where

7 DOLLY COWDERY
Born **27 SEP 1913**
Where
Died
Where

15 JANE
Born

Start your own chart to record the members of your family from
the past. It may be as simple as this, or you can draw it like a tree
or widening circles. Put in each new ancestor as you find him, with
as many facts as you can discover. Each person will have a number, and there will be twice as many branches for each generation.

tracking down your family is to interview all the relatives and longtime friends you can find. Most young people don't realize how important it is to question relatives and friends immediately. Twenty years from now many of them will no longer be here to tell their remembrances. Some will die, others will move away, and still others will completely forget the stories they could tell now.

What you collect from them is only "hearsay evidence," but it provides many valuable clues you can follow up later. Be sure to stick to the facts. Don't let romantic notions of what you think happened take over. In the end, the stories you hear will be more exciting than the ones you could make up anyway. A tape recorder—if the person interviewed does not clam up at the thought of her voice being recorded— will help you recall later any facts that might otherwise be forgotten.

Even the most unimportant-sounding fact may turn out to be useful. Your great-aunt mentions a relative with a French name—Girod.

"I think Girod was a Huguenot," she says, "but no one ever found out anything more about him."

Just because no one has learned much about an ancestor up to now does not mean that *you* can't learn more about him. You have many sources to use now that no one ever had before. Girod's name may be listed in a book called *Huguenots Who Came to America,* for example, or he may be found on a sound-indexed passenger list. No one's case is entirely hopeless—unless you run out of imagination.

Start by questioning an old family member who is good at talking. Always keep in mind working from the *known* backwards to the *unknown* and guide him gradually into the past. Ask about his children

14

and when he was married before you ask him to tell you about himself as a child. You may be surprised how pleased he is to have you interested in his story. Just remember that old people tire quickly. An hour or two at the very most will be enough to corner Grandpa or Great-aunt Mabel.

Don't press too hard for exact details at first. You should not be discouraged if Grandpa does not remember his mother's maiden name. Perhaps he will later. Perhaps he won't, too. You will not get all the answers you want, but you will get some at each sitting and maybe a few good stories.

You are a very important part of the questioning, even though you say hardly anything at all. You are there mainly to keep the conversation going. Your role is important because you are related to the person you are questioning. You represent the next generation.

Be ready with questions to ask if your "memory bank" wanders back through time. But don't fire questions at him as if he were taking an oral exam for his Ph.D. You may need several sessions before you have even the birth dates you want.

When you get vague answers like, "I think my mother was born about the 1870's," just write down "about 1870's" and don't try pinning him down yet. Later, some related date may make him remember and he'll say, "I remember now that her brothers used to call her 'red legs' because she was born the year the red-legged grasshoppers were so bad in Kansas." Later you can look up the year and find that the grasshoppers hit Kansas especially hard in 1876.

There are many things you want to learn about your family besides dates. Here are some suggestions to jog faded memories and to provide clues:

15

"What sort of house did you live in? Did your family build it themselves? Did your father own the land?" The answers could help you find information in land records, mortgage records, etc.

"Tell me about your family. How many lived at your house? Did your grandparents live with you?" This may help you find their address in their old age as well as their wills and death certificates.

"Did other people live with you besides your family?" This could help identify "other people" mentioned in wills or found living in his house during a census year.

"What were your brothers' and sisters' names? Which ones were older than you? Younger? Whom did they marry?" Even though these extra relatives are not directly related to you, their records may help you solve some of your own problems later.

"What was the nearest town like?" You may find more about your family by searching out the town's history another time.

"Who was the first member of your family to come to this country? When did he come and from what country?" You will want this information later, but first you must work back toward the immigrant ancestor, not *from* him.

"Did your family always go to church? Which church or synagogue?" Records in these places can add much to your information later.

"Do you remember anything about your grandparents? Where and when were they born?"

"How did you meet the person you married? What was he or she like? Did you move often?"

"What sort of work did your father do? How did

16

The homesteader had to erect a dwelling to secure ownership of his land. This luxurious one actually had windows

---

This 1895 New Mexico Territory "family" included uncles, aunts, an Indian servant, and the family dog

you decide on an occupation?"

"Did our family have someone in the Revolutionary War? In the Civil War? Other wars?"

Some questions will be planted to get information that you can find in written records. But others you may ask so that you can learn more about the social life of your relatives.

"What were weddings like in your family? Funerals? Holidays?"

"Who made the big decisions in your family—like moving, choosing an occupation, getting married?"

"Who corrected the children when they were bad? How?"

"Did your family have any black sheep?" This one may not be answered.

"Who paid for college educations?"

"Who helped support the old people in the family?"

"Who took care of you when you were ill? What illnesses did you have?"

"At what age did your family consider a person 'grown up' "?

"What do you think was your biggest moment in life? Your lowest?"

Suppose you have just come from your first question session with Grandmother and things did not go well. She started talking about "young people nowadays" and how they weren't like this in her day, and you never did find what you wanted to know. What do you do now?

Give her a rest. Her detour into a discussion of young people may only be her way of hiding a poor memory. Soon her mind will be working and she will come up with an interesting story or a remembered fact for your next visit. Be prepared for one side effect —once Grandma gets turned on, there may be no turning her off. Keep in mind that the remembering is good for her, and you will have some choice stories to pass on to your children.

"I remember my grandfather's name now," said one old man a week after his interview. "They called him Jacob the Hunter." He chuckled and waited for his interviewer to urge him on. You should be prepared to urge when you can sense a story in the making.

This particular Jacob had been well known around his part of the country for his successful hunting trips. Even though they sometimes lasted weeks, Jacob had always returned home with enough game to feed his neighbors and his family of eight children. One time though, he was gone for seven years. His wife and children were sure he was dead. Then one day Jacob returned. He walked in the door, hung his hunting rifle over the fireplace, sat down, and said two words:

"Been huntin'."

It was two hundred years before anyone ever found out where Jacob had been for those seven years. The person who found out was one of his descendants who had been searching for ancestors. Modern advances in family-hunting had turned up two Jacobs with the same last name—one lived with his family in New York and went hunting. And the other lived for seven years in Vermont, bought land, married, buried his wife when she died, sold his land, and disappeared from Vermont at just the same time that Jacob the Hunter returned to his home in New York State.

Interviewing takes patience. Try not to jump ahead to another subject too fast or your informant will think the previous topic has been closed. You may miss the gold nugget that would have made an unusual story—like the one about Jacob the Hunter. Try to get specific details as often as possible.

"I remember your great-grandfather never let anyone in the family leave the table without cleaning off his dinner plate. It was a family custom," said one grandmother.

The interviewer made a note of that family custom and then wondered if there might be more story to it than appeared at first.

"Why was that, Grandma?"

"I always understood it was because of his grandfather. He was in the Revolutionary War, you know."

"Do you remember any more about the story?" The interviewer prodded carefully because too many questions might scare away the memories.

"Well, yes," Grandma finally said. "His name was Ambrose and he enlisted twice in the Revolution. Once to serve his own term and once to serve for his father. Food was very scarce that winter. Ambrose and his best friend had been living for three weeks mostly on apples that were no larger than robins' eggs. Then one day they were both assigned to kitchen duty. They watched the baker scrape dough out of a large bowl to make bread and they managed to look so hungry that the baker offered them each a little wad of dough. Ambrose, smelling the bread baking in the oven, could not wait to eat his piece, so he cooked it at once and ate it while it was still steaming hot. But his friend put his piece in his knapsack, intending to cook it later over an outdoor fire. Later that day his knapsack was stolen, and the friend was so angry that he cried like a baby because he had not eaten the bread when he had the chance. After the war was over, Ambrose told that story to every child who would not finish the food on his plate and I even told it to my children."

Interviewing has its hazards. One of them is the relative who insists that you are a direct descendant of George Washington or some other well-known person. Keep the suggestion in the back—not the front— of your mind. The relative may be right about being a descendant of someone famous (though no one is a direct descendant of Washington because he had no children), but first you must prove that you are related to the famous person. Then you discover you are not alone, but thousands of others can make the same claim. In England in 1783, the Duke of Norfolk thought it would be nice to have a family reunion of all the living descendants of the first duke, who had been killed three hundred years before. He gave up when he found that the first duke now had thousands of descendants and six thousand of them lived close enough to attend his party.

Another hazard is the relative who says you are wasting your time searching for your family because some distant cousin has been working on the family history for seventeen years. Any day now she will publish a whole book filled with your ancestors. First, the distant cousin may have *some* of your family in her book—in which case you will probably be asked to *buy* a copy. But only your own brothers and sisters have exactly the same ancestors that you have. Second, the cousin will have "unknowns" in her book, because there is no such thing as *finishing* a genealogy book. No matter how hard you try, there will always be a few blank lines in your own history.

By all means, write to the cousin, telling her that you are searching for your family and ask if she will help you from the information she has already gathered. You may even be able to help her—by telling her what you have learned from family interviews.

Don't panic when your best friend says her family has its own coat of arms and takes you to see the crest hanging above the mantel. A word of warning about "family coats of arms"—there is no such thing in the United States. Armorial crests that have been brought over from another country were granted to one particular branch of a family—like the eldest son of Edmond Randolph, to be inherited down through the eldest surviving son. Only when you can prove direct descent from the very person who was granted a coat of arms and have a certificate to prove it have you the right to call the crest yours. Anyone can send a clipping from a newspaper or magazine and receive the "Hill" or "Johnson" coat of arms in return, but it is *not* one belonging to your particular family. Such offers are only commercial appeals to vanity. Study heraldry if you are determined to have a family crest on your writing paper.

Everyone wants to be related to someone famous. And you probably are. You may even be related to the famous person that family tradition says you are. Or you may find other well-known persons in your background that no one knew about. This desire to have someone special in your family is not limited to white Anglo-Saxon Protestants. Many black people were told that their African ancestor was a chieftain's son, and just as many Indians believe that they have a chief or a princess behind them.

Don't be too surprised if you find that your nonfamous ancestors are even more interesting and likable than the famous ones. A pioneer who saved his family and lost all his belongings when his raft overturned in an Ohio River rapids may thrill his descendant more than a Civil War general. You may come across some horse thieves, pirates, men who fought on the "wrong" side in the Revolutionary War, and other personalities. By the time you finish this book, you may discover that they were not undesirable ancestors at all.

Arm yourself with plenty of looseleaf notebook paper, because you will find many more ancestors than you expect. Each person should have a page for himself—although some will require several pages. Lined paper is best, because most of your notes will be written by hand. Choose the regular 8½″ × 11″ size so that if you have photocopies made of some notes, all the pages will be the same size. Try to write your notes neatly the first time, because recopying is a waste of time—and also increases the chance of making mistakes. If you come across a name spelling or a word you think is a mistake, you should write it down just as you find it. For instance, if Grandma has written "a fresh coat of whitewash was applied ever year" and you think she really meant to say "every year," you should copy it just as Grandma wrote it with the notation *(sic)* after the word "ever." *Sic* is Latin for "thus," meaning "This is the way I found this word."

Write down everything you learn about each person. Facts you are doubtful about can be written in pencil until proven. Often you will come across one-line squibs like "paid taxes on land in Westmoreland County, 1874" or "Grandma says John Ward and Elizabeth Hawk were married on a rock in the middle of the Potomac River at Harper's Ferry." Some of these one-liners may turn out to be valuable clues

HUSBAND _____

Born	Place	
Chr.	Place	
Marr.	Place	
Died	Place	
Bur.	Place	
HUSBAND'S FATHER		HUSBAND'S MOTHER
HUSBAND'S OTHER WIVES		

WIFE _____

Born	Place	
Chr.	Place	
Died	Place	
Bur.	Place	
WIFE'S FATHER		WIFE'S MOTHER
WIFE'S OTHER HUSBANDS		

	CHILDREN — List Each Child (Whether Living or Dead) in Order of Birth SURNAME (CAPITALIZED) · GIVEN NAMES	WHEN BORN DAY · MONTH · YEAR	WHERE BORN TOWN · COUNTY · STATE OR COUNTRY	DATE OF FIRST MARRIAGE TO WHOM	WHEN DIED DAY · MONTH · YEAR
SEX M/F					
1					
2					
3					
4					
5					
6					
7					
8					
9					
10					
11					

SOURCES OF INFORMATION

OTHER MARRIAGES

NAMES: WATSON, John Henry
PLACES: Sharon, Windsr, Vt
ENTER ALL DATA IN THIS ORDER.
DATES: 14 Apr 1794
To indicate that a child is an ancestor of the family representative place as "X" behind the number pertaining to that child.

FAMILY GROUP RECORD

that you might have missed. Be sure to write down where you find each smidgin of information, no matter how meager it may seem.

Each person should also have a family group record chart that shows him listed with his brothers and sisters when he was a child and another that shows him as a parent, listing all his children. These charts can be made by you from the sample shown in this book or can be bought for only a few cents each at a local historical society or library. The chart described at the beginning of this chapter will help you to see the overall picture—where each ancestor belongs on your family tree.

DATE	LIBRARY CALL NO.	DESCRIPTION OF SOURCE	PURPOSE OF SEARCH	RESULTS
5 APR 75	Vo I 1 R	History of Indiana Cty.	to find Woodend family - Saltsburg	found children, parents, wife of William W. Woodend
10 APR 1975	Vo W 4 R 1975	Hist. Westmoreland Cty.	to find FLACK family	found story of James Flack's capture and escape from Indians
2 MAY 1975		Interviewed Helen Ray	to find brothers' names	got all 9 names – no dates!
8 MAY 1975		National ARCHIVES	to find Joseph Fish's military record	found only request for pay for self and one horse – but may find more in N.Y. state because he was in STATE MILITIA!

One more valuable tool that you will need is your own research chart—showing what books you looked in for information or what relative you talked to and what you found out from each source. Even if you learn nothing from searching through a book, you should record that fact on your research chart to prevent your doing the same work over again. Your research chart should include:

1. Date of your research
2. Name of the book you searched through
3. Book's call number (in case you want to find it again at the same library)
4. What you were looking for (purpose)
5. What you found (results)

If you use a tape recorder when interviewing people, you will not have to stop them while you write down notes but can transfer all the information later from the tape to your looseleaf pages. A camera is another good hunting tool. An interested parent or relative can help with your research, too, if you have enough enthusiasm to fire him with interest for your family search. Besides these tools, you need only unbounded curiosity.

Interviewing the relatives and friends gets the family search started. But sometimes people who can help live far away. That is the time to start writing letters.

If you are the type who writes "Dear Aunt Sally" at the top of a page and then are struck dumb, remember that a letter should sound just the way you sound when you talk. Don't ask so many questions that your letter looks like a final exam, though. Everyone hates tests, and your questions will be laid aside for a rainy day and probably never answered. Try to ask only the most important questions in the first letter, and rarely more than three at a time. Include them in a short, friendly, "visiting" kind of note:

Dear Aunt Sally,

You will be surprised to hear from me, but I thought you might like to know I am starting to gather information about my family history. Any names and dates that you can send me will be helpful, but I especially want to know the names and dates of my grandparents. Do you know when they were married? . . .

Who knows—Aunt Sally may be so pleased to find that you are interested in the family that she'll add you to her will and leave you her collection of salt-water sponges or matchbook covers. At the very least, you will have made a friend. She may even suggest someone for you to write to for more information. Don't panic if you don't know the person. Your letter will be welcome if you make it very clear what you want to find out.

Dear Mr. Doe,

   My aunt, Miss Sally Jones of Breakwater, New Jersey, suggested I write to you because you know more about the Maryland branch of the family than she does. I especially want to ask about the family of my great-grandparents, Abigail and Walter Williams, who moved to Chestertown, Maryland, in 1911. Their son John was the father of my father, Peter Hunt Williams, but I cannot find his birth date, marriage date, or the maiden name of John's wife, Mary. Thank you very much for your help.

Sincerely,

Typewritten letters are easier to read. You can single-space your letter but be sure to leave plenty of space between short paragraphs. Never make it long enough to go over onto a second page. Be sure a return address appears somewhere on the letter and not only on the envelope. But most important of all—enclose a stamped and self-addressed return envelope for the answer to be sent back to you. This return envelope should always be included—even if you are writing your favorite grandmother. Older people especially find it hard to get out to buy stamps for their letters.

   Never write to a historical society to ask them to "find your family." They do not "find families," although they may have a great deal of information about your family somewhere on their library shelves. Many grown people think they can stop in at an archives or historical society someday and ask to see their own family records. Family-hunting is a do-it-yourself project. The only way to get out of doing it yourself is to pay a professional genealogist to find your relatives and ancestors.

Next in importance to questioning people who knew your missing relatives is starting your own family and personal archives. Most adults put important documents like passports, the deed to their house, marriage license, bankbooks, and other valuable family papers in a special—sometimes fireproof—place. But many other papers are archives material for your own collection.

First, there are the "historical" papers that belong to you alone. These may include such documents as your old report cards, school yearbook, scrapbooks, photograph albums, diary, old letters, the hospital certificate from the day when you were born (the one with baby footprints on it is not a birth certificate), and even newspaper clippings about your Little League baseball team or Girl Scout campouts.

You are lucky if you have an attic or a cellar to raid in your search for archives materials. You might even discover something your family did not consider "valuable." One man traced his slave ancestor to a certain tribe in Africa because of an amulet and an old fetish doll he found in an attic drawer.

Old letters belong in your personal archives. You may have read them before, but now that you are searching for your family you may find that a sentence you ignored before actually contains clues:

"Anna's grandmother Lindsay died last week in Pittsburgh. She was 79 years old."

The clues? Since the letter was dated January 28,

You will find many more records to add to your own personal archives

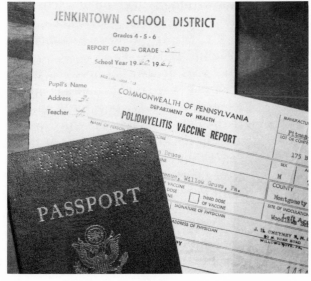

1869, the reader found the place and date of death of her grandmother's grandmother and could make a good guess about her birth year.

What sort of clues are found in an old diary? Names of brothers and sisters, uncles and aunts. Often birthdays of family members are mentioned during the year. And, most of all, you find the personality of the writer and of the people in the diary.

"Little Lester fell out the screen door again today" appears several times in an 1885 diary, proving that the great-grandfather whom a searcher knew only as a very old man was really once a little awkward baby. Another diary, kept by a lady who evidently did not care much for her mother-in-law, reveals some secret desires: "February 13: The old lady was up here to stay tonight . . . tomorrow is valentine *(sic)* Day. How I wish I could get down to the Corners. I would get old lady Mary a valentine that would make her dance a hornpipe if I could find one bad enough for her, but I am afraid that I could not." (In fairness to "old lady Mary" an eyewitness who knew her says, "She was a lovely person. Everyone adored her except her daughter-in-law.")

Diaries do give a one-sided picture, but between their pages are real people speaking in everyday language just as those persons would speak, rather than in the flowery, many-syllabled words that were common in the books and letters of long ago. During the years that "keeping a journal" was popular, people wrote very neatly, so their diaries are not usually hard to read.

Men kept diaries, too, but often they were of a business record. One family hunter found a diary from an ancestor who was a country farmer with a scheme for getting rich quick that included building a bridge

30

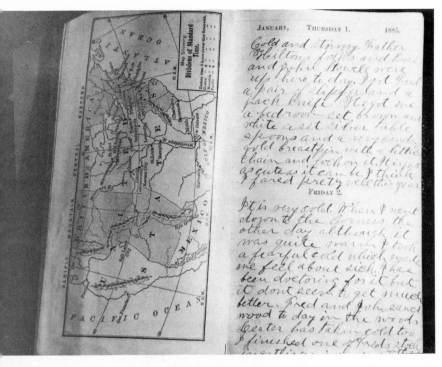

What was she like—the girl who started this diary in 1885?

A small girl's sampler is proudly displayed over 150 years later

over a creek near his land. Collecting tolls on the bridge would make money for him—providing the bridge got built before the local farmers all headed toward town with their produce to sell. His problem was three teen-age sons who preferred fishing to helping build the bridge and whose only ambition seemed to be escaping from work.

There are clues in needlework, too. Sewing a sampler must have been pure torture for little girls who wanted to run outside and play with their brothers, but a sampler provides evidence as factual as a birth certificate.

"Susan Fish's work in the 11th year of her age, 1836," is all one sampler says, but it was enough to make one girl search through her family to find out more about the little girl whose letters are uneven in height and whose single blue flower towers over the trees and a pigeon. Another researcher discovered a friendship quilt in her attic that had been signed by a dozen of her ancestors.

Keeping scrapbooks goes back almost a hundred years. Scrapbooks may be filled with newspaper clippings, dance programs, recipes, old jokes that struck the funnybone of a teen-ager, and some pressed flowers. Many mothers kept a baby book with clues inside about birthdays of the family, lists of relatives and the baby gifts they sent, and names of missing people. Attics often offer evidence that a person lived—in the form of textbooks from school, old yearbooks, a high school diploma or maybe the favorite old book of a person long gone who had scribbled her thoughts in the margins.

Old photograph albums provide dozens of clues—if the pictures are labeled. If they are not, see if you can find someone right now, today, who can tell you

A "silver anniversary" spoon reveals a forgotten wedding date

This 1865 wedding certificate was so pretty that it was encased in a glass-topped table

who the unknown people are. Photograph albums are useful tools to have around when you interview an elderly person. A picture can call forth memories of when and where it was taken. Sometimes dates can be tied in with pictures—like the one of Great-grandmother holding your grandfather in her arms and sitting on the running board of a 1928 Buick.

"We thought she died about 1926," says someone, but here is proof that she did not.

The only book that most pioneering families could carry along on their travels was the family Bible. In many ways, it was considered the "fireproof safe" and in it were recorded the vital matters of a family—births, deaths, marriages. A Bible page is considered a more valuable document if the births have obviously been written down as they occurred and not recorded some years later by someone who might have made mistakes. Different-colored inks and different-looking handwriting for the various events help prove that the entries were made as they happened. Sometimes what is written down is a dead giveaway that the writing was done later. For example, one Bible had written at the top of the page:

"Grandmother Rose married grandfather on May 11, 1824." Then the children were listed in the order they appeared. But it is obvious that someone who was not Grandmother or Grandfather, since they would never have referred to themselves that way—wrote the information down. A family Bible was the standard wedding gift to a young couple starting out their life together, and many families may still have one of these archives around.

Sometimes a house search will turn up all sorts of items that give clues to missing people. A silver tablespoon marked with initials and a silver anniversary

Autograph books often include clues to missing relatives

Heston Bates never dreamed, when his artist-uncle painted his portrait, that someday his descendants would use it as a clue to family history

date reveals the date of a wedding twenty-five years before. A genuine grandfather's clock was sold with its "history" of all the different families that had owned it down to its present owner. A silver Revere bowl has the bride's initials and the wedding date. A coffee table was designed to hold an old-fashioned marriage license under its glass. Years ago, people were often buried without their wedding rings, and the date inside the ring provides evidence of a marriage date. All these help family hunters pin down their missing persons more accurately.

A large manila envelope should be kept for each of your ancestors as you find personal archives for him —newspaper clippings, photos, copies of something valuable like his army record, or other memorabilia relating to that particular individual. This is the way records are kept in the National Archives of each man who fought in one of America's wars under orders of the Federal Government. (Records of *state* militiamen are kept in the separate states.)

Before taking your ancestor hunt outside your home, you should analyze the material you have collected so far. For each person you want to research further, you should have:

1. His name
2. The approximate dates he lived
3. The place he lived

Check through what you have gathered and see if there are any glaring mistakes. One boy who thought his family history had been done by someone knowledgeable found a baby who was born three years after its mother was supposed to have died and a boy who must have become a father at age four and a half, if the dates were to be believed. When your information differs from what someone else has written down, don't be too quick to erase. Cross it out, drawing a line through lightly so the item can still be read. That way you have a record of two differing opinions and you may need to reread the "wrong" information at a later date. Just add your own information with a question mark if you are uncertain.

Collect all your people who lived in one certain area and try to research them at the same time. A boy did not go very far in the old days to find a wife. Often he only walked to the farm next to his or married into the same family where his big brother had found a wife.

The place to start people-hunting outside your home is at the nearest large library. If you have never learned to scan a page quickly, this will be a good time to start. Suppose you are looking in an index and find a reference there to your ancestor John Francis Drake on page 211. Close your eyes and see that name in print in your imagination. Now let your eyes sweep over page 211, *without focusing* on any word. The name John Francis Drake will almost jump out at you with only a little practice. Then, of course, you focus your eyes and read carefully what is said about him.

By now, the one name you had when you began hunting ancestors has turned into several names—all belonging to your people. Soon you will be adding many more to the growing list.

2

Zillions of Names

Prince Khnumenhotep II was not about to go into the next life without having proper roots in this world. But tracing his lineage was made much harder by the fact that his ancestors had lost a few wars. When that happened in Egypt, the victors destroyed the memory of the defeated ones by knocking down all their monuments. At long last, Khnumenhotep's genealogists traced his family back to the gods. Now, where could he put his pedigree to make sure it would never be lost again? Papyrus was too easily destroyed. Stone monuments, such as his ancestors had built to themselves, had not lasted either.

Finally he found the perfect place. When archaeologists broke into his tomb many centuries later, they found Khnumenhotep's mummy surrounded by walls on which were written his impressive pedigree. Above was written: "I have kept alive the names of my fathers which I found obliterated upon the doorways [making them] legible . . . not putting one name in the place of another."

Eventually the top brass in many countries were hiring experts to look up their family trees and make them look good. Julius Caesar told his genealogists not to bother tracing any lowly ancestors if they valued their lives. Sure enough, Caesar was soon found to be descended straight from the gods—a fact that did much for his political career.

Soon all the kings were having their families traced through other kings and straight back to Adam and Eve. But the Esterhazy family of Hungary announced to the world that their family went farther back than Adam and Eve. In fact, they said, the Adam who was in the Garden of Eden was actually the third Adam Esterhazy!

When William the Conqueror invaded England he was shocked to discover that the English had never bothered to give themselves more than one name. All the Norman conquerors had brought along surnames for themselves, mostly names of the castles or towns they had left behind in France. Now they planned to establish medieval fiefs and they had to have some way to keep an accurate count of their vassals. Therefore, the British were all ordered to have last names as well as given names.

Some of them chose to use patronymics for surnames. That meant using the name of their fathers with their own given names. John, the son of Randolph, called himself John Fitz-Randolph because "fitz" means "son of." In Wales, David, the son of John, tacked "ap" in front of his father's name and before anyone realized it, David ap John was being called David Upjohn. A Scottish Highlander put

"Mac" in front and so Gilleain's descendants were known as MacGilleain and shortened to MacLean, McClean, McLane, and all the other ways it can be spelled.

People from other countries changed their names in much the same way. In Greece, "son of" was shown by adding "pulos" at the end. Polish names added "wiecz." In Sweden, Jacob's son called himself "Jacobsson," but a Norwegian Jacob's son became "Jacobssen." In Scandinavia, family searchers can get very confused finding Nils the son of Erick using the name Nils Erickssen, while his son Johan was called Johan Nielssen and his grandson used the name Johanssen. By 1880, even the Scandinavians were getting confused, so they adopted whatever name they were using then and kept it for their family name.

When the Norman conquerors told everyone in England to find a name, some were already stuck with a name of sorts that had been given to them by the people who lived around them. Some names were chosen because of their jobs. The man who made barrels was named Cooper. The blacksmith was called Smith. Every good-sized village had at least one Smith, Carpenter, and Miller, and the Smiths of one village were not necessarily related to the Smiths in the next. Other names were chosen for descriptive reasons. Russell had red hair. Long was tall, and Ballard was bald. When people from one village moved to another, they were sometimes named for the village they had left, so that William from Hilltown became William Hilton.

Names were sometimes changed when people left the Old World. Many French Huguenots turned their names into English-sounding names because they were afraid of being captured. Italian immigrants changed their family names to make them easier for Americans to pronounce and spell. Giuseppi Castiglione became Joe Castelli. Many names were changed because the immigration officer could not spell the name and the immigrant couldn't spell at all. When a German man named Weber pronounced his name as "Vaber," that was often the way the officer wrote it down. Even when an immigrant could write, mistakes were made because of the handwriting. The French Huguenot Nicolas Marteau is still found in many early records spelled "Martian."

If a name can possibly be spelled some other way, it probably will be. Good spelling was not one of the talents of early Americans—even in the 1870's. Those who could write spelled all words just exactly the way they sounded to their ears. Some names can be spelled two hundred different ways.

The minister who married two young people in 1637 could not settle on how to spell the groom's name, FitzRandolph. Written in the church records is this notation from the minister:

Marryed EDWARD FITTSRANDOLFE May 10, 1637 to Elizabeth Blossome. EDWARD FITTS SURRANDOLPH joyned church May 14, 1637, Scituate, Mass. Our Brother FITTSRENDOLFE wife joyned August 27, 1643, Barnstable.

Today there is a way to find a name no matter how badly it is spelled. The Soundex System (sound + [ind]ex) was developed for indexing names by the way they sound. Already the 1880 Census and some passenger lists have been soundexed. Here's how it works:

1. Take the first letter of the name
2. Then add numbers to it for certain key letters:
   a. Add 1 for B, P, F, or V
   b. Add 2 for C, S, K, G, J, Q, X, or Z
   c. Add 3 for D or T
   d. Add 4 for L
   e. Add 5 for M or N
   f. Add 6 for R

The letters A, E, I, O, U, W, Y, and H are not coded. They appear only when they are the *first* letter of the name. Do not code Van, Di, Dela, or Le when they are used with the name. When two of the key letters come together, use them as one letter. For example, a name with two T's together will have only one 3 in the code. A name with a CK will have only one 2 in the code.

The code number for HILTON then comes out H435. And so does the code number for any of the ways it could be mispronounced or heard wrong, like Halton, Holton, Hultman, Halladan, or Holtham. Although soundexing does not solve all the searcher's problems, it at least makes it possible to locate a hard-to-find relative whose name may be keeping him hidden.

A difficult name may take several tries, even with the soundex system. If you still cannot find your person's name, try pronouncing it the way your person might have said it and see how many different possibilities there are. If a name starts with a B, try starting it with a P. Or substitute V for W, just as the immigrant named Weber said his name. When he came through Ellis Island, Johann Wilhelm Mengel was changed into William Engel. Use your imagination wildly if you cannot find your person easily.

The first name of a person often gives clues about

his parents. Puritan families were anxious to break as far away from established churches as possible. The names Mary and Peter were thought to be too Roman Catholic, and Elizabeth and George were too Anglican. Instead they named their children for qualities they could live up to, like Thankful, Patience, Godsgift, Loveday, Honor, Prudence, or, if she was an orphan, Orphana. Remember and Ransom were boys' names, with Ichabod for an orphan boy.

Many colonial families used the Bible to make all their difficult decisions—including what to name the baby. The new father often opened the Bible with his eyes closed and pointed to a word on a page. An appropriate name could usually be found nearby, in case his finger touched on a word like Sin or Evil. Mr. Pond found that there was an element of risk when his finger touched on the page telling the story about Belshazzar sending for Daniel to interpret the handwriting he saw on the wall. The child went through life with the name "Mene mene tekel upharsin Pond." One family hunter was having trouble finding anything about his ancestor whose name was Meshach Potter. A librarian suggested he look instead for Shadrach and Abednego Potter. He found plenty of information about them and also about their middle brother, Meshach.

Often families had several children with the same first name. If little Elizabeth Stone died at three months, her next born sister was given the same name. When she died at two, the name was given to the third daughter born. One Englishman named every one of his sons Edward because he wanted to be sure to have one Edward survive. In this case they all lived—to the lifelong confusion of their parents and friends.

You may discover some strange names in your own background. Storm Van der Zee was born during a storm when his parents were crossing the Atlantic Ocean. That story was true. But when a descendant found one of his ancestors named Preserved Fish, he just could not believe his eyes and so invented a story to go with the name, saying that a baby had been found floating in a basket in the Hudson River by a New Bedford fisherman. He took the baby home and named him Preserved. Although the story sounds fishy, there is a possibility that one of the several men who has carried the name of Preserved Fish could actually have been picked up by a fisherman. One descendant even went so far as to "prove" that on November 11, 1761, Captain Eleazor Gedney and his wife, Levenia, had traveled to Westchester, New York, on business and were returning aboard a sailboat when a terrible squall capsized the boat. Only the ferryman aboard the boat survived and he said that there had been an infant in a basket with the Gedneys. The story, proven or not, is just the sort that appeals to family hunters. But a good genealogist states only the facts that he can prove.

Have you come across an ancestor with a sort of title? Although North Americans steered away from real titles, they still could not help occasionally adding a note of distinction to some people they knew. At first, "Esquire" following a name meant someone much respected, one step down from a knight. "Gentleman" was one step down from an esquire. The title "Goodman" (or a woman called "Goody") meant the person was head of a household. Many other terms did not mean what they mean today. "Junior" and "Senior" were not necessarily father and son. They

Find the names of all the brothers and sisters of your
ancestors. Even their middle names may provide clues

could have been an uncle and nephew who bore the same name and lived near enough to each other that people had to distinguish between the elder and the younger in some way. When "Senior" died, "Junior" often moved up a notch and became "Senior." The term "cousin" was used to cover many relatives and did not mean legally the child of an aunt or uncle.

Having a slightly different name is a help in searching for family. One girl had often been teased because of her long name. She was glad that when she married it would be changed to something shorter than Featheringill. Then she started looking for her roots and discovered her name to be so unusual that almost every Featheringill she came across was one of her relatives. Not only did she appreciate that but also the fact that her name had been shortened by one of her ancestors—from Featheringstonehaugh.

Finding that an ancestor has a middle name is another help. Why go through a thousand references to John Nelson if a person's name is John Reade Nelson and there are only fifteen references to him? At least those fifteen will probably be to the right person. Nicknames often disguise a person's real name. One descendant kept searching for Patty Stowell, only to discover that the woman's real name was Martha.

Maiden names disappear quickly. Women were not given much credit in the old days and they were not supposed to be individuals with names all their own. A man names his wife "Betsey" in his will, but rarely tells her maiden name because to him she lost it when she married. As late as the 1900's, a woman dropped her maiden name completely and if she needed a middle name, she used the middle name she had before she married. When Matilda Nelson Woodend became a McLean, she did not call herself Matilda Woodend McLean as a girl would today, but always signed herself Matilda Nelson McLean. Sometimes, though, a mother was able to preserve her maiden name by sneaking it in as a middle name for one of her sons. Matilda had plenty of chance to do just that because she had nine sons—each of them carrying a middle name that helped trace the female family names back several generations.

For some reason, John Belconger wanted so much to disappear that he even changed his initials. Soon after he married Mary Kelly in Massachusetts, he and his wife moved to a place where he thought no one would ever find him again—Woodbridge, New Jersey. In those days New Jersey was the other end of the world from Massachusetts and today it is almost lost again among the tentacles of interstate highways and turnpikes leading into New York City. John changed his last name to Conger and raised a large family of Congers who eventually produced thousands of other Congers.

To this day, no one has ever proved when John arrived in this country or where he came from. But many of his descendants have theories. One says he sailed over on his own ship, *Elizabeth Anne,* in the 1660's, and since he is not on any ship passenger lists that can be found, that theory is possible. Another claims he was a French Huguenot, but someone else claims that if his name was French, it could not be pronounced the way it is. Still another says his mother's maiden name was Bell and Bell was his middle name. Whatever his secret, John (Belconger) Conger took it with him when he died.

Compared to today's standards of "owning things," ancestors did not have much. They made up for it by having huge families. If you must guess about when an ancestor married, you will be right most often by placing the girl between eighteen and twenty-three and a boy just past twenty. After the marriage, the babies arrived about every two years. A gap of four years between children usually indicates that a baby was born who died very young. It was common to lose babies under a year old. Mothers also died having children. When a mother died, everyone pushed the father to remarry as soon as possible. The result was that many men had several wives, with a set of children to each wife.

The devastating result was that each man may have fathered a dozen or more children. This makes a problem for a family searcher who must first find which child was related to him and then find which mother that child belonged to. One lady wanted very much to prove that her ancestor was the child of a certain man's second wife. His first wife had been nice enough and so was his third. But his second wife was a descendant of kings. The child's birth date was never found. However, she did learn when the child was baptized—making it possible for the child to belong to the second wife. But a child does not have to be an infant to be baptized, so that was not proof. If the child was baptized at three years of age, he belonged to the first wife. No kings. His brothers belonged to the third wife. Also no kings. Ancestor-hunting can be very frustrating to the person looking only for kings.

A cemetery is the best place to collect names belonging to ancestors. If the relatives you interview say your whole family is in the local cemetery, you are in luck. You will find dates there, and in many cases relationships to the people nearby. Take a trip there

MARTIN

EZRA F. 1831–1912
SOPHIA P. 1827–1868
SARAH H. 1842–1877
WILLIAM H. 1873–1873
SAMUEL B. 1870–1872
MARY A. 1872–1879

A boy working for a merit badge discovers six ancestors all at once

with a camera on the first sunny day, but don't take pictures at high noon. Long shadows make the letters on the stones show up much better. If the letters are too hard to read, ask the custodian if you may use a piece of chalk to trace the letters on a dark stone (or charcoal to trace them on a white stone) so they will show up in a photograph. Explain that the stone belongs to your family and you want the picture for your personal archives, so that he knows you are not a vandal.

Another way to take the information from a tombstone is to become a "grave rubber." Take along some masking tape, a large roll of heavy wrapping paper, and a box of large wax crayons—the kind workmen use to mark boards in a lumberyard. Clean the stone with a brush so there are no pebbles, dirt, or lichen moss on it. Tape the paper to the stone so that it fits tightly. Then, after you remove the wrapper from the crayon, rub the side of it over the surface of the paper. Stones made of slate will give the best rubbings. Those of marble and schist will come out the worst.

Tombstone language sometimes needs its own dictionary. "Ae" and "Ag" stand for "Aged," so "Ae 2 yr" means "Aged two years." Sometimes the age is more explicit, like "Aged 2 yr's, 4 m's, 3 d'ys." The word "relict" means the lady was a widow when she died —a handy clue if you are looking for her husband. But if the wording says "Consort of James Howard," you know that James was alive when she died.

Wandering through a cemetery, someone good with numbers will come upon the phenomenon known as "the lost eleven days." James Wilson, the tombstone says, was "born March 1, 1715, and died March 15, 1765, aged 50 years and 3 days." Even a first-grader can see that the man was 50 years and 14

Taking photographs in bright sunlight can make dates hard to read. Slanting rays are best

Grave-rubbing is not only fun but many interesting copies are sold as folk art

WILLIAM HICKS
1734 — 1803

days old. What happened? He was caught by the changing calendar.

The Gregorian calendar had been calling January 1 the first day of the new year since 1582. But the English and the people of the colonies ruled by the English doggedly stuck with the Julian calendar which called March 25 the first day of the new year. For one thing, it was exactly nine months before the birth of Jesus on December 25. And besides, the months had been named for the Julian calendar. September, the seventh month counting the Julian way, was abbreviated "7ber." October and November were written "8ber" and "9ber" on many tombs. Why change things?

But by the year 1752 what had been apparent to astronomers for 170 years was finally becoming apparent to British politicians. Sun time was no longer in agreement with calendar time. If things kept on as they were, winter would soon be coming in July. The calendar had to be changed, with January 1 as the first day of the new year. But by now the British had waited so long to change that in order to come out even they would have to strike eleven days from the calendar in addition to omitting the extra day in leap year three times every four hundred years from then on.

Accordingly, the day after September 2, 1752, was September 14. All over England, people actually rioted because they believed that eleven days had been taken out of their lives. Many people did as George Washington did. He had been born on February 11, 1732, so he just changed his birthday to February 22. Eventually people adjusted to the new calendar, and the change was almost forgotten.

But for ancestor hunters, the calendar change

crops up with *every date falling between January 1 and March 24 (inclusive) during the years before 1752.* Two dates, called double dating, are used for those dates.

When one hunter discovered that his ancestor Mary Randolph had been baptized on March 22, 1656, and his records showed baby Mary had not been born until March 1, 1657, he was tempted to switch the dates around to make sense. Then he remembered the calendar change. It was cleared up by writing the baby's birth date as March 1, 1656/7.

If you trace your family back as far as 1625, you will discover over sixteen thousand people who are directly related to you. That is not even counting their brothers and sisters. They will include people with names you never heard who lived in places where you never imagined you had relatives living.

Now it's time to move to a library for a little indoor hunting. You will meet some eyewitnesses who knew your ancestors when they were living. Just remember that sometimes eyewitnesses are not completely accurate. And also:

Don't believe *everything* you read in print!

3

Finding an
Eyewitness

One little boy walked into a genealogical library in Connecticut and asked for a book about the pope's life. He had been told that this was a special kind of library with people's life stories on its shelves. When he found that the pope's life was not even there, he walked out disgusted with the whole place.

Although you may not find anything on the pope's ancestors, you will find that a genealogical library, or a historical society, or even a small section of your local library that is devoted to genealogy, has a kind of help you need. The size of the collection will determine how much you can find in any one library. A small historical library has books about its own local history and the people who lived in that area. But even the smallest library may have many records on microcards or microfilm that will save you a trip to a larger city or university library.

At first you will be doing what genealogists call "secondary research." That does not mean it's not as important as "primary research." It means that you will be finding information that comes secondhand from another person—a sort of eyewitness telling about the person you are searching for.

Start out for the library with your long list of names—in alphabetical order to save you time. Some people take along their notebook sheets for each person. Others list the names on small index cards because they fit a pocket or purse better. Just remember that everything written on another card must later be transferred to the looseleaf sheet and there is that chance of making a mistake. Be sure to jot down on your research chart what you learned about each person and where you found the information so that you will never have to do the same research twice. Take extra sheets or cards, because you will probably find some new names at the library to add to your family.

Some people have a "thing" about libraries. Does your throat turn dry and dusty in a strange situation because all the people there look as if they know exactly what they are doing? This can happen in a historical library where people sit busily writing down their family notes. The books lining the walls may contain hundreds of stories about your own people, yet you haven't the slightest idea which way to turn first.

If the librarian is not standing waiting for your approach and you are not yet ready to face him or her, wander around the outside edges of the room to get the lay of it. You will see a section loaded with fat volumes of county histories and histories of valleys or mountain regions. This is where you later find out about the neighborhoods your people lived in. Many families are named in them and yours may be there too, but usually these books are not indexed according to the names found in them and you must search for what you want.

As you search through old county and area histories, you'll run into dozens of stories about your people, their friends and neighbors. Many include details about early American housekeeping and home life—like the story about one blue coat worn by nineteen different grooms to their weddings in Westmoreland County, Pennsylvania. Where else could you learn that the sugar camp was a favorite place for young men and women to get acquainted while they kept the fire going all night under the boiling sugar? Or that the only way to kill a squirrel for dinner without ruining the meat was by "barking it"? That meant by aiming the ball between the squirrel and the tree bark. Or that only one letter in a hundred was addressed to a woman in the early 1800's?

On another shelf are what the librarian calls "mug books." They were popular within the past hundred years and almost anyone could have his "mug" put in one providing he had his picture taken by a certain photographer and had someone write up his biography to make him sound important.

Another shelf may contain "scrapbooks" bulging out at the sides with newspaper clippings. Sometimes this is the only place you can find an article when a relative says, "Oh, there was a story in the papers about that family several years ago." Many people enjoyed saving bits of local history from the newspapers, but scrapbooks cost money. For no cost, a person could get an outdated old lawbook bound in genuine leather and paste his news clippings over top of the old legal reading matter.

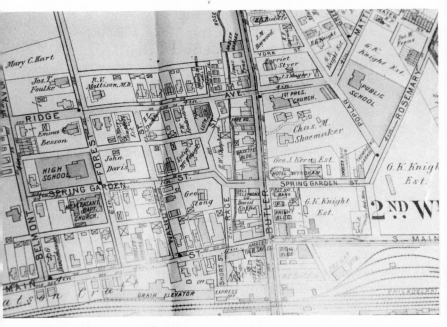

From a plat book an ancestor hunter can often "see" the town his people lived in and even the shape of their house

The library has many atlases to help you locate the exact places your ancestors lived. Some cities and railroads put out a surveyor's "plat book" showing the shape and size of a person's house and lot in great detail. Gazetteers are helpful in telling you where to find your person who lived in a place called Mud Flats, Arkansas, when you cannot find it on a modern map. Old postal directories are used, too, to help find the nearest post office to your person's farm. Then there are books explaining local place names. Perhaps your ancestor lived in "The Glades" in Pennsylvania. There is no such place on today's map, but your ancestors did not see the countryside as you see it today—from an interstate highway. A glade was a large open space in the forest and a Pennsylvania map of 1787 shows "Great Glade" and "Long Glade" between Fort Bedford and Fort Ligonier.

In alphabetical order, you will find the family history books. These are books about certain families, written by nonprofessional people who were once standing in the same muddle you are in now. When they began finding their families, they had so much success, they wanted to record all they found for future generations to read. The books usually have the family name in the title: *Traditions of the Fitz-Hughs, The Oxx Family, Nelson Descendants,* and so on. Naturally you will edge along the shelf looking for your own family name. Then, consulting the list you brought along, see whether any of your "other" names have a family history already written.

You've found one? Now check to see if the person on your list really belongs in this particular family of the same name. If there is an unusual name on your list, see first if there is a book with that name. You can pick up the family histories and glance through them in most libraries. But you cannot take a book out of a historical library. Now you know why all those people are so busily writing!

The librarian is there to help you. But he has a hard time keeping a straight face when adults walk up to the desk and, with a worried look on their faces, say, "Where's *my* family?" Tell the librarian that you are starting a search of your own family. He may suggest that you look in the family card catalog to see whether anything listed there is about your family. It is just like a card catalog anywhere, except that it lists family names. Note carefully that if you want to find something about the Robertson family from northern

New York State, you pass up the Robertsons from other states—at least for now.

The family card catalog may list information you cannot get from books. If you find something under your family name that looks as if it might be your branch of the family, fill out a request slip, writing down the call number clearly. Most request slips also require that the *date* on the card be listed, and it would help to include any other information, such as the state or area, for the librarian. Then you will receive everything filed under that particular number —it may be a box of letters, a manila envelope with an odd assortment of papers inside, or even a half-finished family history done by someone who could not complete it.

Another card catalog will list all the books in the library. This is where you will find family history books. If you do find one with your family name that really has some of your family in it, you are lucky. Since each one is arranged in a slightly different way, you may need to study it a short while to see how this particular family history is designed. Most begin just the opposite way from the way your family search begins. Books start with the "first American" (or the progenitor of the family) who came across the ocean and then follow the family through to the present.

You may find several names after each person, like: CHARLES FLACK (Gilbert[8], Luther[7], Edward[6], Jacob[5], Nathaniel[4], Samuel[3], Nathaniel[2], William[1]). These are not all Charles's names, but the names of his direct forebears. They mean that his father's name was Gilbert, and Gilbert was the son of Luther who was the son of Edward, and so on back to the first one in this country, William. There are two Nathaniels—one who was the grandfather of the other. This system makes it easy for you to trace your own family if you are related to Charles—rather than having to read the whole book to find which man was the father of each.

In addition to having dates and details to fill in your family pages, these family histories are packed with interesting and often exciting stories that have been collected from family tradition—the eyewitnesses. Because they are not scientifically documented, you cannot be absolutely sure they are 100 percent true. But the fact that they are not proven need not lessen your interest in the stories. When you read that a person who was only a name to you a few minutes before was actually a young man who helped capture the infamous commander of Andersonville Prison the day after the Civil War ended, you have to be made of iron not to be impressed. You can be sure of an element of truth anyway and if you are persistent, you may even be able to prove the story by following up the man's war record.

Just because you do not find your family in the title of a family history book does not mean your family is not in the books. Your people may be "buried" in the history of another family. Every time someone got married, another name was added to a family history. So the family names you are searching for may be on the pages of many books. And there is a way to unbury them.

"If only there was an index!"

You will find yourself saying that over and over. Until now an index at the back of any book was probably something you hardly bothered with. Now that you can see a real need for one, there may very well not be any in the book you are reading. Always ask a librarian if there is an index available, however.

Sometimes a person who felt just as you do now sat down and made an index for a particular book for his own use and left it with the librarian.

One very important index is called *The American Genealogical-Biographical Index.* It contains over a hundred volumes now—and there are more to come. Names are listed in it in alphabetical order—names that have been found in family histories, lists of soldiers, newspapers, and in many other places where you might never have found them.

Suppose you are looking for a Benjamin West who lived in Maine about 1912. Run down the list of Wests until you come to *West, Benjamin.* It's all right to notice that there were Benjamin Wests in the 1700's and 1800's, but you are looking for the one who was in Maine in 1912. When you find him, copy down the list after his name. Those are places where he is "buried." One of the places may be in a book that is not in your library. Copy its title, and the librarian will tell you where you can find the book.

You may see a notation in *The American Genealogical-Biographical Index* after your person's name that looks like this:

Transcript: 31 August, 1908, 136;
10 Sept 1913, 3547

That means you will find something about him in a column that appeared in the *Boston Transcript,* a newspaper of many years ago. It does not matter that so many years have gone by. For your purposes, the older the date, the better sometimes. The information given in 1908 may be something that you could no longer find today—like information taken from a gravestone marker that has disappeared since 1908.

Ask the librarian if you may look at the *Boston*

Transcript on microcards. Rather than shuffle through stacks of newspapers, you can go through cards, where the column has been photographed in miniature. You read them through a machine viewer that magnifies them. Find the card dated August 31, 1908, and run down the column until you reach item 136. You will find that someone had written to the newspaper on that day with information about the very ancestor you are hunting. His information may not be 100 percent correct, but there is truth in some of it, and for the first time your ancestor comes "alive."

The *Boston Transcript* has not been published for over thirty years and yet people read its genealogical column every day! The column began in 1876 with just a series of questions and answers. People asked things like, "Is the letter *f* in golf silent?" Golf was a brand-new sport then, and how else could one learn how to pronounce it in the days before radios? But almost at once, people began writing to the column for help in finding their missing persons.

"Does anyone know of a Pole by the name of Alexander Bulkowski who died in Boston or elsewhere in Massachusetts? He is supposed to have been a man of property," asked E.L.P. on June 6, 1886. Probably E.L.P. was much more interested in what happened to Bulkowski's property than he was in the man, but soon all the questions in the column were from people hunting and finding ancestors.

For over fifty years, people sent in items about the ancestors they knew and asked about the ones they could not find. Each inquiry was given a number so that when another person wrote an answer, it could be printed under the same number. The best part is that today we do not have to wait two weeks for the answers. They are on the next microcard.

Suppose you are looking for Hannah Conger. You look up her name in *The American Genealogical-Biographical Index*. There you will find several listings. By the time you have read them all, you know quite a bit about Hannah that you never knew before. You have found that (1) her name was really Johanna, (2) her parents were John and Mary Conger and were the original settlers in Woodbridge, New Jersey, (3) there is a good chance that John's name was changed to Conger from Belconger when he moved to New Jersey, (4) her father owned land in New Jersey on March 18, 1669, and (5) Hannah's daughter was born December 7, 1666. Now you have a whole new set of clues to track down.

Although there is no longer a *Boston Transcript* column, some other city newspapers have genealogical columns once a week. Some companies publish a periodical with the same sort of information. One of these is *The Genealogical Helper* published every other month in Utah. It contains articles about family-hunting in various parts of the world as well as pages of family inquiries with people trading information. For a few dollars, you can put in a "Wanted Ad" for one of your missing people and hope to get answers from the readers.

The New England Genealogical and Historical Register is another collection of news columns about missing families from the New England area. Its volumes cover a very large shelf, but it includes a good index. Even though you live in Kansas and believe you have no relatives at all in New England, you may still have ancestors from there. The ships from the Old World landed on the Atlantic Coast and unless your ancestors went straight to Kansas, they passed through the Eastern States and left a trail behind them during the early years in this country. People whose ancestors passed through Pennsylvania, stopping to raise a family for a generation or two before moving west, may find their names in the volumes of *Egle's Notes and Queries,* also with an index.

Ask the librarian where to find the "compiled lists." These books will come in handy once you know more about your persons. There are lists of California pioneers, early settlers in Georgia, Scotch-Irish and Germans in Pennsylvania, and thousands more. Well-known ancestors can be found listed in biographies like *The American Catholic Who's Who, Who's Who in American Jewry, Who's Who in Colored America, Who's Who in the Central States,* to name just a few.

There are literally dozens of magazines published about genealogy. The New York Public Library gets six hundred a year. Each state has at least one magazine on genealogy in that particular state.

If you had asked one of your early ancestors where he lived, he would have answered "In the Connecticut River Valley" or "In East Jersey in Piscataway Township." Pinning most of them down to a city or town was hopeless, because most lived in the country as farmers. To them, the important part of their address was their county or township, and you have to think as they did in order to find them today. Often the "big town" they lived near is found on today's road map in the smallest, lightest print. It was probably on a river, the main transportation route of those days.

As soon as you find several ancestors who lived somewhere near each other, take a road map of the area and lay a piece of onionskin paper (or other paper you can see through) on the map. Trace the rivers

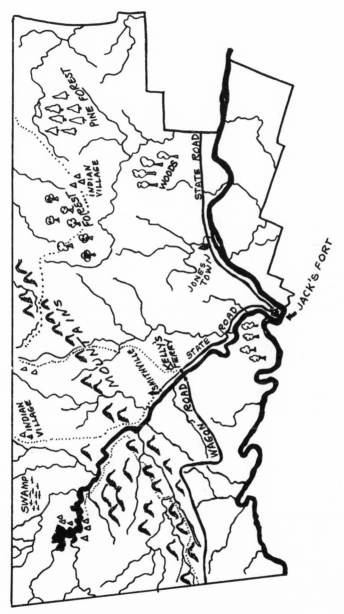

Small streams of water and any hill that meant a climb for a horse
and buggy were important to your ancestors' way of life

first. Then put on it only the towns where you had ancestors living. If there are mountains high enough to slow down a horse-drawn carriage, add those to the map. Now you have a good idea of how their world looked. Your best chance of finding how the world looked to your person in 1795 is to find a 1795 map of his area in the library. Then keep the map nearby when you read about your person's neighborhood in a local history book.

Counties are not the same today as they were long ago, however, and so you need another library helper called *The Handy Book for Genealogists,* by George B. Everton and Gunnar Rasmuson. You need this book for ancestors like Alexander McClean, whose home can be found on the map in Adams County, Pennsylvania. But if you read the Adams County history, you will not find him—because when he lived in the late 1700's, his home area was part of York County and his story is in the history of that county. And his records will be found in the county seat of that county also.

An old city directory, dating from the year your person lived in a city, can give you more information than the modern telephone book. If you know he lived in the city of Philadelphia, look up his name and you may find it listed with his address. Try to find a plat book made about the same year, so that you can "see" the shape of his land as well as the names of his neighbors. City directories came out every year, so you have plenty of chance to find your person listed one year at least. Also, after his name you will find his occupation. A city directory can also help you locate the main buildings that were in a town that year. Suppose you had an ancestor buried in Steubenville, Ohio, in 1880. Today Steubenville is a large industrial city, but then it was a pleasant country town. You know that if you could find your great-grandmother's tombstone, you could get the information you need for continuing your hunt. But where would it be? The old Steubenville city directory mentions only three churches and *one* large burial ground. That is where you start hunting.

You may not live near a library that has any genealogical material. Then what do you do? If you are thinking of writing a letter to one, asking for your family history, forget it. Historical societies are always getting letters from children like this one from a sixth-grader:

Dear Sir,

Please send me everything you have on Colonial Philadelphia. I need it for Mr. Thompson's Social Studies on Friday.

Librarians cannot possibly help Mr. Thompson's social studies class. Not because they have no information about Colonial Philadelphia, but because they have far too much. They do not print freebie pamphlets or look up information for people. They will not help people like this writer who has genealogists mixed up with mind readers:

Dear Sir,

I am doing my family history and need to know everything you have about the Harvey Smith family.

That letter writer was told to keep her letter brief. But there is such a thing as too brief. No dates—no city or state—not even a clue as to *which* Harvey Smith family. The whole family? There may be a dozen Harvey Smiths ranging from 1624 to 1976, all living in the same county. There may even be several books about families named Smith, each one of which has its share of Harveys. And the letter did not even include a "Thank you for your trouble."

The kind of letter that a historical or genealogical society will answer is one that asks a specific question that will take no more than a few minutes to answer. "Have you a book entitled 'The Smith Family of Northfield, Massachusetts' or 'The Descendants of Harvey Smith' on your shelves?" Then the library will reply that the book either can or cannot be found within its walls and perhaps will tell you the library hours during which you can read it. Or you could ask whether their family card catalog includes a listing for "the Harvey Smith family who lived in Northfield, Massachusetts, between 1780 and 1812." *Always* enclose a self-addressed, stamped envelope with any request to a librarian.

If you really want information from a historical or genealogical library badly enough to pay for it, you should ask the librarian how much it would cost to have a professional searcher (called a genealogist) do the searching for you. A genealogist knows exactly how to go about finding missing people—although each ancestor is different. Some are harder to find than others. But, as a rule, the genealogist can come upon clues in minutes, whereas it might take you hours. You will pay by the hour for this know-how, so if you cannot afford to pay and still want very much to find out about an especially difficult ancestor, get a detailed "how-to-do-genealogy" book from the library and find out how the professionals do it. Val D. Greenwood's *The Researcher's Guide to American Genealogy* tells exactly how to do a professional job yourself.

A word of warning: if you are doing your family

history as a part of extra credit for a high school course, don't plan to hire a genealogist to earn your credit for you. You *can* do it yourself. But searching takes time—even for a trained person. Your teacher may not realize this, unless he has actually searched for his own family. Be sure that your work includes a list of the places where you *did* find information as well as the places where you looked and *did not* find any. Otherwise your teacher will have no idea how hard you worked on your project.

One of the largest and most important genealogical libraries in the world is in Salt Lake City, Utah. The chances are very good that some of your missing persons are listed in its vast records. And it is as close to you as the nearest postage stamp.

Although this unusual library belongs to the Mormon Church, its services are extended to everyone— not just to members of the Church of Jesus Christ of Latter-day Saints. It exists because finding and identifying all the members of one's family is a very important part of the Mormon religion. To locate their missing ancestors, they use the scientific methods of genealogy. Young church members begin in the primary grades to learn about their families. They may join a Sunday school class when they are twelve and begin learning how to search through libraries and records, just as you are doing now.

So that people can locate hard-to-find records, Mormon missionaries have traveled all over the world, photographing birth, death, and marriage records, parish registers of various churches, census returns from other countries, land grants, and records of cemeteries and wills. They did not limit their photography to people who belonged to their church, but put all records they could find on microfilm.

69

Genealogical Society, Church of Jesus Christ of Latter-Day Saints

Records of your missing persons may very well be stored
in these tunnels under a mountain of granite in Utah

Positive copies of the microfilmed records are in the library and can be read on a viewer. But the negatives are stored in a vault that would have been envied by the builders of the Great Pyramids. The vault, containing six rooms of floor-to-ceiling storage files, is beneath a granite mountain near Salt Lake City. The ceiling over the record storage room is seven hundred feet of solid granite. Temperature and humidity are carefully controlled to preserve the films. Entrance is through three tunnels, each one guarded by bank vault type doors that are too heavy for even bombs to harm.

Fortunately the files are very carefully indexed and you may find whether any one of your ancestors is listed by sending a request form to:

The Genealogical Society
50 E. North Temple Street
Salt Lake City, Utah 84150

To get a request form (called a TIB form—for Temple Records Index Bureau), write to the above address and ask for a few. Or you can buy them for a few cents each from a genealogical supply house. If you ask The Genealogical Society to find too many people at one time, you may receive a small bill for the service. However, there is no charge if you ask for just two or three at a time.

The TIB form asks whether you want to see an index card or an archives record. There are about thirty-eight million index cards and if you receive a copy of one showing your ancestor, notice that in the upper-left-hand corner there is a "P" or a "C" or both. This notation means that your person can also be found in the archives records as a parent (P) or a child (C). So your next request will be to see that same person as a parent or a child in the archives. In all likelihood you will learn more about him as a child, since you are probably still going backwards and searching for the names of his parents. His record as a parent will show the names of his children. But be patient. It will take six to eight weeks to receive an answer from The Genealogical Society.

A visit to this special library starts on the first floor at the Reference and Orientation area. There trained people will show the newcomer where to find the information he seeks. This is a library particularly knowledgeable about the ways to help young people and amateurs in the art of ancestor-hunting. However, even they will not do the work for you—only show you how to do it.

In addition to browsing through the open stacks that include thousands of family histories, magazines, and histories of towns, counties, states, and countries, the visitor can also look through the family records that more than 6 million church members have gathered on their own families—many of whom may also be related to you. Although this one large library is unique, there are 135 branch libraries in Mormon churches of the fifty states, Canada, Mexico, and New Zealand where you can ask to see certain records from the main library through interlibrary loan.

Since so many valuable records are on microfilm, you should know how to work the microfilm reader before using it at a library. Take only one roll of film out of its box at a time. Many do not have the titles marked on the reel itself and thus are very easily mixed up. When you have finished with the film, do not try to return it to the drawer but let the librarian put it away. Try to have as much information as possible before you ask to see a certain film, because microfilm is not easy to read. You may have to plow through several pages of old-fashioned handwriting before you come to your person, and reading a fast-moving reader can make you as seasick as a fishing boat.

The librarian will show you first how to load the reader. Put the full reel on the right side, taking care to snap it in so that it catches. Then the film slides gently over a roller, between glass plates, and over another roller onto the empty take-up reel. Now, snap on the light switch at the side of the reader and begin winding the hand reel. Soon the film will begin rolling past on the "floor" of the reader. If it is upside down or sideways, you do not stand on your head to read it, but grasp the mechanism at the top of the reader and turn it gently around to the opposite from where it was when you were loading the film onto the reels.

You will probably not begin your searching on page 1, except to look for some sort of heading. If you are looking at a census record, you may see the county name. If the county is the one you wanted to search through, then find your township and begin reading the lists to find your person. However, many counties may appear on the same reel, so you must turn the handle, moving the film forward quickly, until it has reached the county you are looking for. Train yourself not to focus your eyes on the material while it is moving.

Most microfilm readers are the same, but you will come upon some that are more refined with extra-good focusing. You may also find a microfilm printer-reader. This is to be used when you want to print an inexpensive copy of what you have finally found.

The trip to the historical library or genealogical section of a large library is what really gets your family search under way. Don't put it off because you are afraid of having too little information. There is so much new to discover there that a whole day could be spent looking through its unusual books. And sooner or later, if not the first day, they will all come to your aid.

4

Problem People
and How
to Find Them

Some records are much harder to find than others, as a Georgia man discovered when he could not find proof that he had been born sixty-five years before and was eligible for social security. His mother, who had died when he was born, could not help—or could she? He finally proved his age by struggling in to the social security office with his mother's tombstone in his arms.

Trying to find your family may be an easy road or one full of potholes. The going may be especially hard if:

1. You are adopted
2. Your family is split by divorce
3. You have native American Indian ancestors
4. Your family has Puerto Rican ancestors

5. Your people immigrated to the United States later than the year 1880
6. You are trying to find a black slave ancestor

You should begin your family search exactly as most people do, but work a little harder questioning relatives, old people who knew your family a long time ago, and anyone else who can tell you about your family. You may have to work a little harder at it, but finding your own family is worth the effort.

If you are adopted, you must face the question of whether to follow the family line of your adoptive parents, who have always felt you are theirs and belong to their family, or whether to begin the struggle to learn about your natural parents' families. Since a great deal of the information you need for the latter search is not available to you before you reach a certain age, you may be better off to find the genealogy of your adoptive parents first. You will learn many skills in family-hunting that will make the natural-parent search easier when you have more maturity.

Mary Lou Roman (not her real name) discovered at seventeen that she had been adopted. For the next fourteen years, she could think only about finding out who she really was. Mary Lou realized that most of the people she knew who had been adopted did not feel as she did, but she could not help herself. She wanted to know who she was and she felt that she had to find out. She could not get her birth certificate, because only Alabama, South Dakota, and Virginia will allow adoptees over eighteen to see birth records, and she had been born in Pennsylvania.

Luckily, her adoptive parents were very understanding. They knew that she did not want to find another mother and father to replace them. She just needed to have a hereditary background.

Piece by piece, Mary Lou began putting together the puzzle of who she was. The hospital where she was born told her only that her mother was Polish. When she wrote for birth records, she was told that none could be found. Then she joined a group called ALMA (Adoptees' Liberty Movement Association), which was made up of many people who, like her, had the same drive to "find themselves." One of her new friends suggested that she write to the Bureau of Vital Statistics and ask for "a full and complete copy of my birth certificate before it was amended." Within two weeks, she had a name and a mother, Victoria, and a sort of address, Edwardsville, with no state mentioned.

Finding an Edwardsville on a New York State map, Mary Lou and her husband planned a business trip that would take them through that town. But first they had to go to Wilkes-Barre, Pennsylvania, where they spent the night at a motel. Absentmindedly, Mary Lou turned on the television. A commercial was on, so she ignored the message until suddenly she heard the name "Edwardsville." Until then, she had not known there was a town of that name in Pennsylvania. Now she learned there was—and it was only a few minutes from the motel! On that day, Mary Lou and her husband met a woman who had known her mother. Victoria had remarried, had a son, and then died. The search was not over until Mary Lou found her half-brother, just by piecing together clues in the same way she had located her mother.

Divorces often leave families so bitter that the child who lives with one parent can learn very little about the family of the other parent. You may not even know there is bitterness until you try to find the "other" side. Try to convince your parent that you want only to find your roots, not strike up a friendship with the missing parent. Sometimes an aunt or a grandmother can supply information. If there is still too much opposition, perhaps you must wait a few more years.

Official records of every divorce or annulment of marriage are available *where that event took place.* Some states keep them in the Bureau of Vital Statistics, but since each state is different, you can find the proper address in a booklet that you can order from:

Superintendent of Documents
U.S. Government Printing Office
Washington, D.C. 20402

It costs only about a quarter and is called *Where to Write for Divorce Records, United States and Outlying Areas.* The "outlying areas" include American Samoa, Canal Zone, Puerto Rico, Guam, Trust Territory of the Pacific Islands, Virgin Islands, St. Thomas and St. John.

If you are searching for a family of native American Indians—or even a branch that includes Indians —start by studying everything you can find out about the tribe. What were their marriage customs? Did a married couple live in the boy's or the girl's village? How did they name their children, and how can you tell which people were related? Where did the tribe of your ancestors live and what were the migration patterns of that particular group?

Unless you are an Indian in good standing with your tribe, you will probably receive no help from the tribal fathers. That must be done by a personal visit

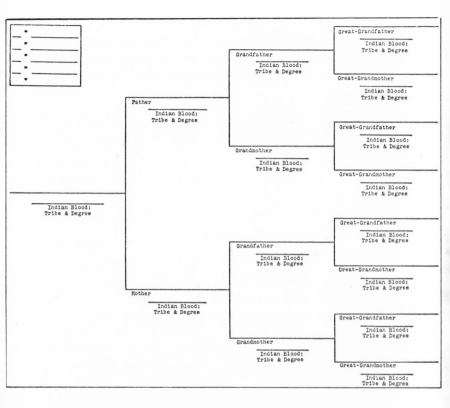

and cannot be done by a white person who is not related to the tribe. Some of the old tribal fathers have memories trained to recite family or tribal history. You may learn that your tribe has such a historian when you are questioning your relatives. Some councils or clans keep written tribal records as well, dating back to 1920. Some tribes, like the Cherokee, Chickasaw, Creek, Choctaw, and Seminole tribes have records back to the 1820's.

Your first task is to find out which tribe your Indian relative belonged to. Then find out whether he was full-blooded, half Indian, or quarter Indian. You must

Apache leaders are shown at a rest stop on September 10, 1886, as they were being taken into exile in Florida. Natchez sits in the front row center beside Geronimo and his son who wear matching shirts

trace an ancestor back to his own tribe in order to get any help from the tribe.

The records with the most information are those from churches and the Federal Government. Church records may go back to the 1500's, when the Roman Catholic Church was christianizing Indians in the West and Southwest. Federal Government records include removal records, tribal enrollment records, annuity rolls, land allotment records (when Indians were given land to settle on), the census rolls, probate records when Indians were named in wills or wrote wills, and school census records and school reports. Most of the Federal Government records are found in the National Archives or the Federal Records Centers, although land records and wills of Indians may often be located at the local office of the Bureau of Indian Affairs. More information is in an inexpensive pamphlet called *Major Genealogical Record Sources of Indians of the United States* available from The Genealogical Society, 50 E. North Temple Street, Salt Lake City, Utah 84150.

Indian names are especially hard to trace. Rides at the Door, the son of Lone Pity and Yellow Owl Woman, is grandson of Chief Bull and Spring Water (father's side) and Screaming Owl and Dry Good Woman With the Coat (mother's side). Often an Indian had several names during his lifetime. You may be lucky enough to find your Indian relative on a census roll that lists his Indian name as well as his English name. Every year after July 1884 the census was taken of Indians who belonged to a tribe under federal control, but this did not include all Indians. Neither did it include those who were only part Indian. Many of those are found on the white census.

One of the easier Indian tribes to locate is the Cherokee. During the 1830's and 1840's, many Cherokees went to Oklahoma. Others stayed in North Carolina and more moved into the Appalachian Mountains so that they would not have to be moved west. Those who went are organized as the Cherokee Tribe of Oklahoma. Their records are at the Bureau of Indian Affairs, Muskogee Area Office, Federal Building, Muskogee, Oklahoma 74401. The records of the Eastern Band of Cherokee Indians of North Carolina may be found at the Bureau of Indian Affairs Cherokee Agency, Cherokee, North Carolina 28719. But there are no particular records of the third group who went into the Appalachians.

George Morrison Bell, Sr., never remembered hearing his parents speak about his grandparents. Then one day after a long illness, he had extra time to spare, so he decided to try to find his Cherokee ancestors. He knew he was hooked on family history by the time he found his four grandparents. In four more years, he had located 97 relatives. His father was one-fourth Cherokee and one grandparent was 15/32 Cherokee. Yet Bell had to go back to the 1760's before he found his first full-blooded Indian ancestor. Fortunately for other Indian hunters with his problems, he wrote a book, *Old and New Cherokee Indian Families,* about his search. Another book, by Emmet Starr, *Old Cherokee Families,* may also help you to find Cherokee ancestors.

Early settlers thought the way to civilize Indians was to send them to schools. One Indian school in Carlisle, Pennsylvania, kept very good records of all the boys who studied there. The records, telling the boys' Indian and English names as well as their degree of Indian blood, are kept in the National Archives. But Indian schools did not solve Indian problems. When the Virginians tried to send Iroquois children to a school, their chief, Canastego, answered very politely:

Our ideas of education are not the same as yours. Our young people who went to colleges and were instructed in your sciences came back bad runners, ignorant of every means of living in the woods, unable to bear cold or hunger, knew not how to build cabin, take deer, kill enemy, spoke language imperfectly. They were neither fit for Hunters, Warriors, or Counsellors. Totally good for nothing. To show our gratitude, we invite you to send us a dozen sons of the gentlemen of Virginia and we make men of them.

Puerto Rican researchers should begin the same way anyone else does—with a hunt through the family, relatives, and friends from the old country for as many clues as possible. There are no naturalization papers of Puerto Ricans, because they all became citizens collectively, the same as Virgin Islanders, Hawaiians, and Alaskans.

For a copy of a birth or death record, you should get in touch with the:

Identification Service
Commonwealth of Puerto Rico
322 W. 45th Street
New York, N.Y. 10036

Enclose a self-addressed, stamped envelope with your request for each record. You can visit the office in person if you live nearby. Records of births or deaths before July 22, 1931, have been moved from small villages to the Division of Demographic Registry and Vital Statistics, Department of Health, San Juan, Puerto Rico 00908. Records since 1931 are kept in Santurce.

The feeling of "plenty of room for everyone" made Americans friendly from the very first toward strangers who immigrated from other countries. However, about 1880 thousands began arriving on every boatload. If your ancestors came then, try to learn as much as you can about the group of people they came over with.

Were they German? Over one third of Pennsylvania was German-settled by 1776. A large group of students came when the German revolution of 1848 failed. Or were your people among the 800,000 Irish who came when a mysterious blight hit the potato crop in Ireland one October night in 1845? Another mysterious blight forced thousands of Greeks to leave their land between 1900 and 1920. Most of them planned to work here and send money home to their families, so only the healthy young men came. But many of these married and decided to stay. Or did you have an Italian ancestor who hoped to come here and farm—only to find that most of the cheap land was already gone, so he joined his countrymen in tenements in the nearest city? You may even trace your family back to some of the Mexican cowboys who roamed the open ranges for generations. Suddenly the land they roamed belonged to another country and they found they were strangers in a land they had always thought of as "theirs."

Whatever you find out about your particular ethnic group will help you locate your problem people. Often a whole town in America was founded by immigrants who had come together from the same village in Europe. The occupations they chose once they were here often reveal where they came from. For instance, if you are not sure what part of Italy your Italian ancestor came from, but you know he was a coal dealer or an iceman, the chances are that he came from Apulia. If he was a knife grinder, try looking around Campobasso for other ancestors of your name. But be sure you know what your European

These immigrants have only to pass the inspection of the
doctor at Ellis Island—then they can enter the New World

ancestor's original name was!

Many immigrants Americanized their names. Some did it on purpose. Others had simplified names handed to them by immigration officials who could not find out how to spell the foreign-looking names. Usually the immigrant could not write, so he could not spell it any better himself. For many others, changing their names slightly was just another step toward becoming an American. A Polish Zaborowski became Zabriskie and Sadowski became Sandusky.

As you get to understand your immigrant better, you will find many characteristics that influenced what he did on this side of the ocean. A Polish family might have been extremely poor, but a backyard (no matter how tiny) was important to them. The Scots, who were used to the fighting between the Highlanders and the Lowlanders, invariably settled on the outskirts of the wilderness, where the battles with Indians were not much different from the battles they had been used to. Because the Scots had had their fill of landlords, they avoided the southland, which was already filling with plantations and a new kind of landlord. While the Greeks held off filing for citizenship because they had planned to return to Greece eventually, other people, like the Swedes, filed to become citizens almost at once.

The immigrants who came last, after World War II, were the quickest people of all to shed their alien skins and blend in. These were the displaced people who could not return to their own countries behind the Iron Curtain. Many of these people applied for citizenship papers the very same day they landed in the country. They never did collect in ethnic groups, but moved in singly and became Americans in a hurry.

In addition to many books written about your particular ethnic group, there are books explaining how to send for vital records in the old country. In some cases, records had been taken from a country before it was invaded, so even they may be found. No case is completely hopeless. A book called *American Origins,* by Leslie G. Pine, tells how to send for records in foreign countries and trace your family there.

Only one immigrant group came unwillingly to the New World. Black people who had been kidnapped from their homes or sold by their enemies into slavery must have had hopes, at first, of escaping and returning home. Slavery was not new to the West Africans. Most of them had seen black slaves put to work in their own tribes after a rival tribe lost a battle. Often those slaves had escaped or had even become respected in the tribe—and so these kidnapped blacks had hopes for themselves.

Their hopes began to fade during the terrible voyage away from their land. Then when they were sold to the first master as soon as the ship docked, they knew there was no hope of returning home. Their families were split up and not even friends were sold to the same master. Then too, every slave was well marked by his own color. This new land was filled with people of a different color. When the new master took them to his home, they found they did not even speak the same language as fellow slaves on the plantation.

If you are related to one of these African slaves, you will hardly be able to rest until you find him or her. But don't buy a plane ticket to Africa tomorrow. There is much searching to be done in this country first. Start tracing your family exactly the way every

87

other searcher does, working backwards from yourself. While you are interviewing relatives and friends, try especially to learn what tribes your immigrant ancestors came from. Since everyone has several immigrant ancestors, you will probably find that you are descended from several tribes. Read everything you can get your hands on about each tribe. As soon as possible, attach each branch of your family to its own tribe and then remember what you have studied about that particular tribe when researching that particular branch of the family. You will be better able to catch any clues an immigrant ancestor left behind when you know something about his tribal customs.

Most of the slaves came from the forested coastal belt of Africa. The Fanti, Ashanti, and Akim tribes were from the Gold Coast. The Ibos (also spelled Eboes) came from the delta of the Niger River. The Mahis, Popos, and Fidas were from Dahomey. Records from slave ship captains and from slave auctions usually included the names of tribes represented by the slaves, although the people sold never were given African names in the records.

Not all slaves came from the coast, however. Often caravans of black men would travel long distances from central Africa. Six thousand men would leave home with a peaceful group of traders, but on the trip back, two thousand would be missing. These men had not deserted. They had been sold by the caravan leaders to the "man thief" and those Africans were never seen again. The "man thief" had instructions to choose dark-skinned blacks, because they were supposed to tolerate the hot sun well. Young people brought higher prices than babies and older people. Do not blame your American-African ancestor if you find no clues from him. He or she may have been no more than a child when carried away from his country.

What sort of clues could a person leave—when he could not write or even speak the language spoken by the others around him or her? Don't worry—your ancestor managed to leave some. Sometimes the clue was a lullaby or a chant taught to the family. One man taught his children the words he knew for everyday objects—the river, the trees, stones, musical instruments. Body movements in a dance, a favorite herb recipe handed down for generations, a drumbeat rhythm sounded unconsciously while thinking about something else, family superstitions, an amulet fashioned for a special purpose—keep your eyes and ears open for these clues that you may never have realized are peculiar to your own family. One girl found an old family journal describing the burial of an infant belonging to an early ancestor. From the details, she found that it corresponded to burials in one particular Gold Coast tribe. The very best clue your person could have left is his African name—because a name tells much in Africa.

Africans do not know very much about black Americans, just as black Americans do not know much about their ancestral homeland. Felix, a Dahomey native who drove a taxi for a living, met his first black American. From him, Felix learned for the first time what had become of the natives who had been stolen from Africa. He had always known that his ancestors became wanderers in order to escape "the Aguda," the raiders who stole black men and who took them away where they were never seen again. Those missing men were all listed in Felix' tribe and every year a ceremony was held for them.

Food was put out for the dead because the missing men were believed to have returned to their native land after death. The black American had known that his ancestors believed also in their return to Africa after death—but it had never occurred to him that the belief was so strong it was working two ways.

Why is it so hard to trace your black family? First, because the families were separated so often. Slaves had been taught never to fall in love, because they could not be sure of keeping their families together. Even the kindest master did not think of his slaves as human. His will might give Liddy, the family cook, to his daughter's family and Ben, Liddy's husband, to one of his sons. A slave marriage ceremony—even though performed by a minister—stated: "You will be true and faithful to her and will cleave to her only so long as God in his providence shall continue your and her abode in such place as you can conveniently come together." To keep slaves in line, their masters often threatened, "I'll put you in my pocket," meaning he would sell them. Most dreaded of all was being sold to a trader, because that meant going farther south and farther from the hoped-for freedom.

Another reason why it is hard to trace black families is the mixture of white blood. Some scientists say 31 percent of the African people in the United States have white blood in their veins. White masters and overseers realized quickly that lighter-colored slaves brought a higher price in the market than pure-black ones. Many areas in the United States have towns of people with mixed blood—the "Jackson whites" of New York, the Moors and Nanticokes of eastern Delaware.

You may find that your black ancestors intermarried with Indians. Blacks and Indians got along well as a rule, because they had a common enemy. Many times black people were used as interpreters and pacifiers when early western explorers had to deal with unpredictable Indians. York went with George Rogers Clark to the northwest and Jacob Dodson, a free black, went with Frémont and Kit Carson to California and Oregon. Jame Beckwourth, a runaway who became a tough frontier scout, even became a chief of the Crow tribe. Many blacks intermarried with the Cherokees of North Carolina. The Roberts Settlement in Hamilton County, Indiana, was founded by such a group. That community supplied many lawyers, dentists, teachers, ministers, and soldiers who fought in the Civil War.

Free black ancestors can be hard to find, too. Children of Northern blacks were often kidnapped and sold in the South. Even adults were kidnapped. On the fifteenth of August, 1801, several free Negroes were offered jobs in Delaware mowing grass and chopping wood. A small sailing vessel was supplied to take them down the Delaware River and up a small inlet. There, instead of finding jobs, they were seized, tied up, and carried in covered carts to Chestertown, Maryland. They were sold to Georgia traders, but this time a suspicious Maryland sheriff looked at the bill of sale and threw the whole lot into prison. The blacks were able to prove they were free men and the kidnap ring was broken up. But there were others to take their place. Nathan Cannon, a free black, was bound when he was sixteen to a man who was to teach him a trade. A bound man was not a slave. But the man sold Nathan one night to another man, and soon Nathan disappeared into slavery.

You may discover a slave ancestor who escaped, like the descendant of Henry Brown. Henry's narrative was one of those published by the Abolitionists. At first Henry's life was tolerable because he knew nothing different. When he was a little boy, he actually believed that his master was God.

"Go inside now," his master said one day. "It's going to thunder."

And sure enough, it did thunder. At age eight, Henry had no doubt that it was his master who had made it thunder. At thirteen, he was sent to work far from home. Then he married and there were little children when his master decided to sell his family away from him. For the first time Henry seriously considered escape. If he were free, he could earn money to buy his family back. So he talked a friend into nailing him in a box and sending him to Philadelphia, to an Underground Railroad address, via Adams Express. The trip was painful, but he survived —and from then on he was known as Henry Box Brown.

Where are some of the places that a black family hunter can look for his people, in addition to the regular places to find family? Considering what an ugly business slavery was, a surprising number of records have been kept.

Plantation daybooks kept a running account of all the plantation activities and they mention many slaves by name. This is a place you cannot look until you know the name of the plantation and your slave ancestor's name. One lady whose name is Bridger learned more about her white ancestor one day at her office. When she discovered that a man named Bridger was on the telephone, she asked to speak with him to see whether he was related to her. She told him what part of the South her ancestor was from and what plantation he owned. Then there was a little awkward pause. Finally the man told her why his name was Bridger, too. His earliest American ancestor had been known as Big Black John. After the Civil War, when Big Black John was freed, his former master Mr. Bridger—who was actually the lady's ancestor —had given his name to Big Black John.

Emancipation records offer another place to look. Also slave registration records. In Pennsylvania, for example, no child born after 1780 was supposed to be a slave. Sometimes though a slave owner sent his female slave to another state to have her child, so the baby would not be born free. After 1788, the births of slave children had to be registered to keep masters from selling infants into slavery and also to keep them from moving expectant mothers.

Land record books have recorded in them the bills of sale for the buying and selling of slaves. Auctioneers kept sales charts that sometimes included the given Christian names of slaves, except those records of slaves who had just arrived in this country. Christening records for those slaves allowed to attend a church often listed slave godparents as well as the family of the baby. Many slaves were considered valuable enough to insure, and sometimes policies can be found with your slave ancestor listed.

If you know who your slave ancestor belonged to, you can often find him or her listed in the master's will. When General Thomas Nelson of Virginia died, he gave "Aggy" and her children (with the exception of her oldest son, Charles) to his son Thomas. "Melinda" was given to another son. Each son was to take "ten hoe negroes and five plough negroes" and each one was to choose a Negro boy to be put to work with the carpenters to learn a trade. But 1789 was to be a year to remember for a black man named Smith

Henry. Not only was he to be given a good house to live in, a good suit of clothes, two shirts, two blankets, three hundredweight of pork and five barrels of corn each year for life, but "he be considered from hence forward as free and discharged from all service."

Have you followed an ancestor's trail toward Canada? The Fugitive Slave Act was passed in 1850, and from that date no slave was safe in any Northern state—even though he had risked his life to escape. Slaves heard all sorts of talk, like: "There are guards at every street corner in Washington, D.C." In 1852, 30,000 black people fled to Canada.

In the library, be sure to check the card catalog under these headings for information on black people:

"European War 1914–1919—Negroes"
"U.S. History—Civil War—Negro Troops"
"U.S. History—Revolution—Negro Troops"
"U.S. History—War of 1812—Negro Troops"
"U.S. Army—Negro Troops"
"Women, Negro"

There are many reference books that may help, too. Ask where to find *The Black Information Index, Index to Periodical Articles By and About Negroes, Who's Who in Colored America, Black American Biography, Black American Scientists, Black Americans in Public Affairs,* and *The International Library of Negro Life and History.* Be sure to look also under "Historical Biographies."

As with other families, the best place in the census to begin looking for a black family starts with the 1850 census, when families were first listed with all their names. Censuses in the years after 1850 included even more information.

FRANK LIGHTNER, Sr.
DAPHNEY LIGHTNER
DR. J. A. LIGHTNER
JOHN A. LIGHTNER
FRANK LIGHTNER, Jr.
CALVIN E. LIGHTNER
PRESTON LIGHTNER
RAYFORD LIGHTNER

ETHEL LIGHTNER
LEATHIA LIGHTNER
GLADYS LIGHTNER
LAWRENCE T. LIGHTNER
ALLEN LIGHTNER
HERBERT LIGHTNER
JOSEPHINE LIGHTNER
EVELYN LIGHTNER

Courtesy Dr. Annette H. Phinazee

A proud family posed for this portrait many years ago. One of the young boys became mayor of Raleigh, North Carolina

One help in finding a black ancestor in the census records is the custom of putting a B for black or M for mulatto after a person's name. Finding a black family in a city plat book is easier, too, because of the custom of restricting black people to certain areas of a city. The custom was certainly discriminatory, but it is definitely helpful to the genealogist. Birth, marriage, and death notices for "free persons of color" can be found in newspapers of the eighteenth and nineteenth centuries. Some newspapers, founded as early as the 1850's, were Negro-sponsored. Black people can be found on the voting lists, before the disenfranchisement of the Negro in 1838. They can also be found on tax lists, and much can be found in the National Archives on black people who served with the armed services. Nothing is impossible. Don't ever give up looking.

Writer Alex Haley did not give up. The search for his African ancestor is in his book *Roots.* When Alex was young, he used to listen to his elders in Tennessee talking about their "furthest back person," a man they knew only as "The African."

At sixteen, the African had been kidnapped and brought to this country on a ship to Naplis. There he had been sold to a man named John Waller and taken to a plantation in Spotsylvania County, Virginia. The African escaped three times, but the fourth time, his foot was cruelly cut off across the arch. Now he was considered crippled and his value was so low that he was not sold as the other slaves were. For that reason, he and his wife, Bell, who was the plantation cook, stayed at the same plantation for many years. He was called Toby, but he made his friends call him Kintay. He taught his daughter, Kizzy, all the African words for tree, rock, sky, river . . . words that she passed down to her son, George, and that George taught his seven children. George's son Tom was sold to a man named Murray on a tobacco plantation in North Carolina, where he married Irene, the plantation weaver. They also had seven children—the youngest of whom was Cynthia, who was Alex Haley's grandmother in Tennessee.

"Grandma pumped that story into me as if it were plasma," says Haley now. In a way it was—his very life's blood. After he had written *The Autobiography of Malcolm X,* Haley had an increasing desire to look for his black origins. He had only the few words as clues.

The African had said he lived on "Kamby Bolongo." In the lobby of the United Nations, Haley stopped Africans and asked what the words "Kamby Bolongo" meant to them. One day a man mentioned a Belgian professor who had written a book about African villages and had a knowledge of several tongues.

Haley flew to Madison, Wisconsin, to see the man who had become an expert on African oral history. From him, Haley learned that the word *ko* his African ancestor had used for a guitar-like instrument could have come from the Mandingo word *kora,* meaning a stringed instrument. The sound he had learned that meant "tree" was what the Mandingos called a certain type of West African tree. *Bolongo* meant river and the "Kamby Bolongo" could only be the Gambia River.

Within a few days, Haley was in Africa, with a friend from Gambia as a guide. The Africans there seemed only mildly interested when he said "Kamby Bolongo" meant the Gambia River. Didn't everyone know that? What did excite them was the word "Kintay," the name the African had used for himself. They told Haley that the oldest villages were named for the families that founded them centuries ago. There were some with the "Kinte" name.

For the first time, Haley learned about "griots." They were men of a tribe who were actually walking, living archives of oral history, and they could be found especially in the back country and older villages. Each griot had been trained carefully to recite the history of his village and to teach succeeding generations his art. Each village had its team of trained historians—each ten years younger than the next. They were ages sixty, fifty, forty, thirty, twenty, and a teen-ager in training. Each man was an expert in the story of a major clan. Modern people cannot imagine what the human memory is capable of—but this is the way history was recorded in the days before writing and printing.

When the griot was found who was the expert on the Kinte family, Haley was back in the United States filling himself with African studies. He had to organize a safari to go to see Kebba Kanga Fofana, his family historian, in the village of Juffure. Haley had never imagined himself in charge of a safari—but here he was with a river launch, a lorry to carry supplies, some bearers, three interpreters, and four musicians to play the required background music to the history recital.

The person reading Haley's book does not have to be black to feel the thrill Haley felt as he faced the group to which his ancestor had belonged. Every man was jet black. They had never seen a black American, so their surprise was just as great as his. The old griot, who was seventy-three rains of age, talked for five hours with stops for the translations. Then came the part Haley had waited to hear.

"Omoro had four sons, Kunta, Lamin, Suwada, and Madi. About the time the king's soldiers came, the eldest of the four sons, Kunta, went away from this village to chop wood and was seen never again."

"I had goose pimples the size of marbles," said Haley.

But Haley's search did not end in Africa. He checked the date "about the time the king's soldiers came" and found that a Colonel O'Harris had come to the Gambia River to guard the Fort James slave fort in 1767. It took Haley seven more weeks to track down the ship, the *Lord Ligonier* under Captain Thomas Davies. It had sailed to Annapolis, Maryland, the "Naplis" of the African's story, and arrived on September 29, 1767. In the tax records in Maryland, he found that 140 slaves had left Africa and 98 had arrived alive. He found a newspaper advertising "fresh slaves for sale" on October 1, 1767, "the following Wednesday at Meg's Wharf in Annapolis." He checked legal papers and found that John Waller had sold "one Negro man slave named Toby" to William Waller on September 5, 1768. Then he stood on the dock at Annapolis, Maryland, exactly two hundred years after the African had been sold—and there were tears in his eyes.

Haley hopes to start a black genealogical library, called the Kinte Foundation and named for his African ancestor.

5

Getting In Deeper

Baby Sara was only a few months old on the last day her family was together. Her father had ridden his horse into the nearest town twenty miles away to buy supplies. When he came home, he found his wife and the three older children dead in the cabin. Only baby Sara lay quietly in her basket.

There were no signs of a struggle. The heartbroken father could see from the filled buckets that the family had been to the spring for water. After he buried his family, he took Sara in his arms and rode to their neighbor a mile away.

"They must have drunk poisoned water," was his only explanation. Then he rode away, still in a state of shock. Sara never saw her father again, but she never gave up hoping that someday he would ride into the yard, put his arms around her and say, "I am your father."

Sara grew up with the neighboring family, but they could tell her very little about her parents except that they had come from "somewhere in Ohio." Even then, her adopted family were not sure whether the child's family had come originally from Ohio or whether that had just been a stopping place on the way farther west. All her life Sara tried to learn more. But in the end, she did the only thing she could do— she told her children and grandchildren her story and asked them to pass it along. Today her great-great-granddaughter has a much better chance of finding Sara's lost family than Sara ever had.

Some families are much harder to find than others because they intended to be hard to find for reasons of their own. Losing one's identity was very easy in the days before there were social security numbers to keep track of people. A man could just move into a new area and change his name. Since there was little communication between the frontier and back home where a man was well known, he could live the rest of his life forgetting who he used to be. But there are ways you can try to find him.

Up to now your search has turned up several stories and dates that were told to you by other people— your relatives, the people who wrote local history books, eyewitnesses outside the family who have run across interesting tidbits about your ancestors. The information you have collected so far is what genealogists call "secondary research."

Now you need facts. Primary research is the getting of information from a person or document directly connected with an event. You do not need an official-looking paper with a state seal on it to "document" a fact like the date your grandmother was born. That can be "documented" with a page from a family Bible where her name was written down the day she was born. Or a page from her father's diary saying she was born that day. Or a letter from someone who was there and mentioned her birth date. Perhaps the date on her tombstone is assumed to be her proper birth date. But if none of those is available, you may have to find a copy of a vital record for proof.

Vital records are those showing that a person was born, married, or died. Often these records give other information too about a person. When this country was young, records were not thought to be very important. It was not until later that government officials realized just what information should be on records. For that reason, the later the date on a record, the better information it will carry. You can learn when a person was born from his birth record, but you can also get the same information *and more* from his death certificate.

To find a person's death records, you must know when and where he died.

Finding where he died may be a problem because an old person who lived in the same place all his life may move in with a married son or daughter to spend his last years. Start searching for the children who lived nearest to him. Or if you know where he is buried, see whether he moved in with a child living near the grave site. Because transportation was slow and plodding in the years before trains, the chances are that a person is buried in the same town where he died. His death records will be found in that state. At the back of this book are the addresses to which you can write, in the states and areas, for birth and death records.

What do you do about ancestors who lived before

This hand-painted Pennsylvania Dutch document shows that Henrich Muskenug was confirmed in the Lutheran church in 1769. Was his name Indian?

the states were keeping birth and death records? While some of the New England records go back to the 1640's, the Southern and Midwestern states did not keep vital records until after the 1880's. Those early vital records will probably be found in county and town offices instead of in state capitols.

Vital records of a person who lived in a large city are often in the city archives, in the town hall or city hall. City archivists are usually very friendly and happy to lift down the books a searcher needs to look through. But this search can be tedious, and you should have a good idea that the information you want is there before you start reading through the huge archive books. Be sure your ancestor did live within the city limits when he was born or when he died. The events are usually written down in the exact order when the information reached the city archivist—and not always on the exact day the event happened. A busy doctor might report an event the next time he was in the city, thus throwing off a birth or death date by a few days.

If certificates seem too cold and impersonal and you want a little more personality for your ancestor, try looking him up in the newspaper. After you've gotten the exact date of death from his records, find a newspaper from the town nearest to where he lived. Obituaries (death notices) are especially flattering and will often make your "recently dead" ancestor sound like the pillar of the community that you always imagined him to be. But don't believe everything you read in the newspapers.

Your person may have left clues about himself in the cemetery records or in the undertaker's books. His tombstone can give more hints about his life. Check out the graves nearest his to find any children you didn't know about, or perhaps an extra wife or two. His tombstone may even give his birthplace in another country. An unusually large number of tombstones in a cemetery that said "from County Antrim, Ireland" gave one searcher a clue she had not expected. She discovered that her ancestor had come over with a whole boatload of neighbors from Ireland to settle a small area known as Antrim Farm. Their sons and daughters intermarried and she found dozens of relatives all in the same cemetery. Sometimes the verses on the gravestones tell the story themselves.

> Life is a cheat
> And very soon show it;
> I thought so once
> But now I know it.

Did Joseph Barge write that for his tombstone? Or was it written by his wife, the only one left in his family? The graves next to Joseph's show that one day in September his newborn baby died and two weeks later their year-old son Titus died. A month later, the grave of their 7½-year-old son was dug, and soon after, Joseph, age forty, was buried. No wonder Joseph's wife, standing there all alone, felt cheated.

Marriage and baptismal records can sometimes be found in churches. But not always. Some churches kept records more carefully than others. Often the minister considered the records his own property and took them with him every time he moved to another church. Find out which church your ancestor belonged to before asking to search through the church register.

Marriage records are filed in the place where the marriage occurred. They should be either in the vital

105

statistics office of the state or in the city, county, or town office where the couple were married. A list of places to write for marriage records is given at the back of this book.

Marriage licenses, though, are not the only way of checking on a marriage. Some churches had their young people publish banns, or announce their intentions to marry, for some weeks before the wedding. This gave the couple a chance to change their minds or gave someone else a chance to object. When the girl's father objected, because she was a minor or because he did not like her boyfriend, you may find that the marriage took place in another state. In the Southern states, a boy got a "marriage bond" (another possible record for you to find) to prove that he was free to marry.

The date that a marriage license was issued is not to be confused with the wedding date. John Ward got a license on May 1, 1822, but it was more than two weeks before he could persuade Ann McClean to marry him.

To find a person's birth record, you must know the place and date of birth and the parents' names.

Records of births are on file in the state or place where the event happened. Many people think these records are kept in the National Archives, or at least in their local historical society, but they are not. They are in the vital statistics offices. People who live nearby can go in person to get a certified copy of a birth (or death) record. Those who must write for them will find the addresses at the back of this book.

Another way to find your person is to look for his name in the census lists. When you read the census and find his name there, you feel as if you had just knocked on his front door! A great-grandmother who suddenly dropped out of sight in 1829 was thought to be dead, until the 1850 census discovered her hale and hearty, living with her son-in-law, and helping to raise his motherless children.

Starting in 1790, the U.S. Government sent people around to "take the census" every ten years. At first the Government did not know just what questions to ask, so it simply listed the name of the "head of household" (invariably a man) and recorded the number of males and females in the house, with their approximate ages. There is not much information for the family hunter there.

But in 1845, Lemuel Shattuck designed a census to be taken in Boston, Massachusetts. It was such a good one that the Government asked Shattuck to design the 1850 national census. He probably was not planning to help you in your hunt for your roots more than 125 years later, but his census and those following it can do just that.

Starting with the 1850 census, every person living in a house is listed. The family of Robert James, 31, a Kentucky preacher whose property was worth $2,100, includes his wife, Sarelda, 28. Then there are his boys, Franklin, 10; Jesse W., 4; and the baby Susan, 9 months old. Four-year-old Jesse James and his brother had not yet crossed the paths of any gun-toting sheriffs.

In addition to the name, age, and sex of each person behind the door of the house, there are columns to show whether the person is white, black, or mulatto (which included everyone not pure black or pure white). Often the space is left blank if the people were white, but a B or an M is given for persons of color. This is one time that the prejudice of those days is

GENERAL SERVICES ADMINISTRATION

ORDER FOR COPIES-- CENSUS RECORDS
(SEE REVERSE FOR EXPLANATION)

DATE RECEIVED

IDENTIFICATION OF ENTRY

CENSUS YEAR	STATE OR TERRITORY
COUNTY	TOWNSHIP OR OTHER SUBDIVISION

MEMBERS OF HOUSEHOLD *(List head of household first)*

.NAME	AGE	SEX	NAME	AGE	SEX

INSTRUCTIONS

Use this form to order a copy of a census entry as described on the reverse side. Fill in as completely as possible. Do not send money with this order. We will bill you $2.00 if we provide you with a copy of the census entry requested. Use a separate form for each entry, i.e., family unit or household. Mail to:

Census Records (NNC)
National Archives (GSA)
Washington, DC 20408

REPLY

CENSUS ENTRY REQUESTED:

☐ ENCLOSED ☐ NOT FOUND ☐ NOT SEARCHED *(SEE REVERSE)*

☐ SEE ATTACHED BILL.

☐ SEE ENCLOSED FORMS/LEAFLETS.

☐ A REFUND OF $_____ ☐ IS ENCLOSED.
☐ WILL BE SENT BY THE TREASURY DEPARTMENT.

CASHIER	MICROFILM PUBLICATION	ROLL OR VOLUME NO.	PAGE
	SEARCHER		DATE SEARCHED
	RECORDS SEARCHED		

Print or type your name and address (including Zip Code) within the date below

GSA FORM **7029** (REV. 9-74)

The form you send to the National Archives for copies of a census record from 1790 through 1880

helpful to a person searching for a black ancestor. The professions (most of the people were farmers) are listed for each male over fifteen. If a boy was not working by age fifteen, he was probably listed at the end under "deaf, dumb, blind, insane, idiotic, pauper or convict."

You can get an idea of your person's wealth by the value of his land. Education (or the lack of it) shows up in the column that lists the number of family members over age twenty who could not read or write and how many in the house were attending school.

The people who asked the questions in the census were chosen because they could "write a nice hand." Ability to spell had little to do with it. When a poor speller met up with a person who could not read, write, or spell, the resulting information was such that it is often confusing to the searcher. Try pronouncing the name aloud before you start searching for it. Then if you can think of any other way to spell it, keep in mind both spellings as you read through the lists.

To find a person in the census, know first the county and the township where he lived.

Even though fewer people lived in America many years ago, there are still too many names listed in a county for you to read in a few hours. Know what county your person lived in that particular year—because counties changed boundaries. If you know the nearest small town, try to find out the township too. Sometimes the place called Scrubgrass Township at that time is Fairfields Township today. Use an old gazetteer to find the name of the township in that particular year. Don't bother reading the census lists until you are fairly certain where your person lived.

When using the census, the searcher works from the present back into the past. If your ancestor lived between 1790 and 1870, start with the most recent census first. The person is easier to find when he is older, and the census is better in the later dates. Once a missing person is found in the census for a particular year, you may find him in other years.

When the first census takers knocked on the first doors, people were suspicious. They thought the census was being taken to make it easier for the government to tax them and they wanted no parts of taxes. Others thought it was for building an army and most men wanted no parts of that, either. So their answers were sometimes evasive.

Even though the federal census was taken every ten years, the women interviewed seemed to grow older only by seven or eight years between censuses. Their husbands, however, aged alarmingly fast and sometimes grew older by twelve or fifteen years between censuses in their hurry to get past military service age. This is another time you cannot believe everything you read.

Census lists for the entire country are on microfilm, so that most libraries can now afford copies. The National Archives has branch offices in Boston, Bayonne (for the New York City area), Philadelphia, Atlanta, Chicago, Kansas City, Fort Worth, Denver, San Francisco, Los Angeles, and Seattle. Schools and libraries can arrange to borrow microfilms from their nearest branch office of the National Archives on a regular interlibrary loan.

There is an index to only one census—the 1880 census has been soundexed. Not all the facts are listed under each person's name, but a searcher can at least find the name without worrying about misspelling.

The form you send to U.S. Department of Commerce, Bureau of the Census, Pittsburg, Kansas 66762, when you want hard-to-get copies of the censuses from 1900 to now

Then, having found exactly where the name is and the person's address, the searcher can find it quickly in the regular 1880 census book. The way to soundex the name you are looking for is in Chapter 2.

A mortality schedule is a list of the people who died during the year just before each census was taken. Doctors were worried about the epidemics of typhoid and other diseases that killed so many people. No one knew about germs before 1880 and diseases were blamed on anything from dancing and kerosene lights to the wrath of God. So in each of the years 1849,

111

1859, 1869, and 1879, there was a special census of dead people, listing how they died. Diseases were evidently not the only causes of death, as some listed were: "grain of corn in windpipe," "kick of Hoss," "Penewmony," "machinery wore out," and "Shot dont no hoo done it."

The Federal Government was not the only census taker. In many in-between years, some states made census lists. For the family hunter they were often very good records—like those of New York and Kansas. But not every state has a state census. Only federal censuses are in the National Archives, except for some copies on microfilm of various territories before they were states. State censuses are found in the various state libraries.

The 1890 federal census has been mostly lost through fires. The federal census records from 1900 to now are still considered "confidential" information, and hunters cannot use them for family research except in special cases. You can, however, use state censuses for the twentieth-century years.

Many hard-to-find people may turn up in court records. Ancestors went to court more than most people go today. They went there to become naturalized citizens, to argue over the size of their property, to adopt or take over guardianship of children, to make their wills, to change their names legally, and to pay their taxes. In colonial days, they even had to go to court because they had not gone to church regularly or had used profane words.

Every time they went to court, they left behind some record to be found. William Cowdery and his neighbors went to court because the Iron Works at Lynn, Massachusetts, was polluting the river. It seems the factory did "stop fish from coming up to refresh and relieve the people and something should be done to remedy the matter." The year was 1675.

To find a person's will, you must know when and where he died.

One of the best places to find a person is through his will. Country people were very careful to write wills, because they owned land and wanted to leave it to their heirs. Soon after a person died, his will was probated. That means someone filed a petition (another court record you might find) to have the will "proven." This was a necessary step before the heirs could inherit anything. Sometimes they waited discreetly for about a month, though more impatient heirs may have filed the petition immediately after the funeral. Often instead of a date of death, you will find the date when a will was "proven," meaning he probably died shortly before.

The person who was appointed as executor of the will then had to gather together all the property owned by the man. (Women, as a rule, owned only the clothing on their backs in the days before 1880.) Then an appraiser decided how much all the property was worth.

William Cowdery was considered "a man of property" when he died in 1684. He left to his son "all the land hee lives upon and the pastur and for [4] Passels of Meddow that lieth upon Ipswitch River" as well as "half my house and homstid with half my Meddow upland & Pastur & two thirds of my orchard and half all other of my Goods within Dores and without Dores that I have not Given Away Before to my wife." In addition to leaving his animals to his wife (thus making certain that the son who owned the pasture and the wife who owned the animals would remain good

113

friends), he also left her many items that today's wife considers are already hers:

> 1 featherbed and bolster, a green rug, 4 pillows, 3 cotton blankets, 3 pairs coarse flaxen sheets, 5 napkins, little tablecloth, 2 pewter dishes, half bushel of brass, old kettle, firing pan and warming pan, 3 old chairs, chest and box, pair of cast andirons, little flock bed, book called Faith and Love and also 1/3 part of all the provision for vitell [food in the house].

Old Tabitha was a widow when she died without bothering to write a will, but the appraiser decided her property was worth 81 pounds. Some of her more valuable possessions included:

> a silk crepe gown and pair of stays
> 1 silk handkerchief
> 1 riding hood
> 1 bed with coverlids, sheets,
>   1 pillow with cases
> 1 old looking glass worth 1 £, 6d
> 4 glass bottles
> 1 brass kettle and cooking pans
> 200 boards and 2 books
> ½ part of a cow
> a wooden keg and 2 cider barrels
> some silver buttons

Wills are filled with clues, like the names of a person's children. Sometimes you can even tell how well a father got along with his children by what was left to them. However, in many families, the eldest son received twice as much as the other sons. He was also left with the responsibility of caring for his widowed mother and for educating his younger brothers. Wills can also be misleading. In the old days anyone related to a person might be referred to as "my cousin." Often grandsons were called "son" and so were sons-in-law. A will might mention land owned in other areas. Land owned across the sea might indicate where your person came from originally. He may also leave you clues as to his religion (leaving money to a church), his profession, or his military service.

Wills are filed in the county where the death occurred. But in some places wills are in the county probate court, while in others they are in the county superior court.

To find a person in land records, know when he lived and where he owned land.

Almost everyone owned some land when it was cheap and there was plenty to spare. This means that researchers often can find their person in the land records (when they bought the land) or in the tax records (when they were taxed for it). This is one time when "more recent is better" is *not* true. Older land records have more information than recent ones.

Just the description of Sam Haines's property in 1664 contains material for several family hunters. His property was "beginning at a hemlock tree between Haines and Francis Drakes near Captain Champernoones Creek, from thence 72 rods west to the cartway at the fence between Goodman Haines and Walter Neal, thence 192 rods due south to a pine and thence 72 rods to a pitch pine tree east, and from thence to the hemlock just above named." Obviously there would not be much point in looking for the boundaries of this property today!

Persons who bought land from the U.S. Govern-

115

ment will be in records found in the National Archives—but only if they were the first owners of that land. Land that had been owned by someone else and bought by your person will be recorded in local town and county offices. The records fill volumes, so be sure you know as much as possible about your landowner before searching.

When you finally do locate your person on some land records, you may learn a good bit more about him. Often his wife's name is listed and sometimes the names of his children as well. Deeds also give the address of your person and, in a case where he bought the new land while he was still living somewhere else, may even mention a previous address.

You can keep a close watch on your ancestor's life by reading his tax records. Although income tax is fairly new and you cannot find those records, you can find the times when your ancestor paid taxes on his land and other property. In 1778, John McFeely of Cumberland County was a farmer with two horses and four cows. By the next year, he was listed as a blacksmith and had only two cows. Perhaps he hated farming. Or the community needed a blacksmith and he had a skill that was useful.

To find your person's naturalization record, you must know the date and place where he swore allegiance.

Every researcher has many immigrant ancestors—one for each branch of the family—unless you have some pure-blooded Indians in the family. So why aren't naturalization records a wonderful source of information for family hunters?

Before 1776, immigrants were not considered immigrants. They were mostly English men and women

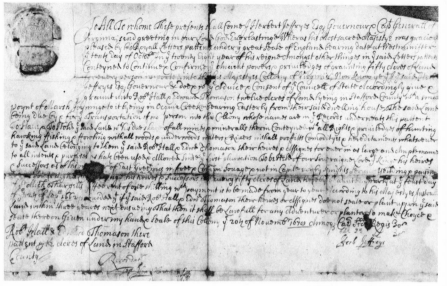

The oldest document in the National Archives is for 12 acres of land in Virginia in 1678

Abraham Lincoln is not often remembered as a soldier—but he received this bounty land of 120 acres for service in the Illinois Militia

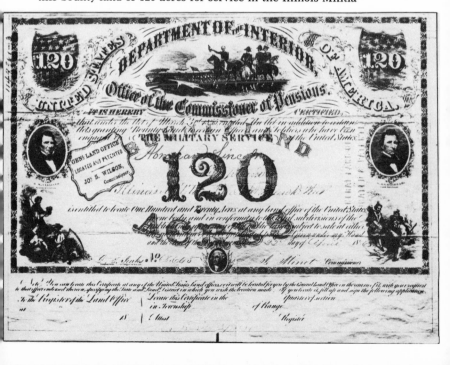

arriving in an English colony. From then until 1868, most immigrants just signed a statement of allegiance when they got off the boat. After that year immigrants swore allegiance in a courthouse, and that is where the records will still be found—up until 1906 when the Bureau of Immigration and Naturalization was established by Congress. Records since 1906 have some information in them, but they are still held confidential for at least seventy-five years.

Although you may be breathless now with places to look for your roots, this is by no means the end of the line. For every door that closes in the face of the searcher, there is another one that can be opened. Read some of the books included in the Bibliography for many more ways of rooting out hard-to-find ancestors.

6

Should We Bury
This One Again?

Never be ashamed of the truth or your ancestors," says one genealogist. "After all, who knows how they might feel about *you?*"

Sometime during your search you are sure to come across a few people who do not measure up to your expectations. Before you bury them again and pretend they are not yours, try to understand something of the conditions under which they lived.

A descendant of Hannah and Josiah Owen was horrified to discover that they had been whipped and forced to wear the letter "I" (for incest) sewn on their sleeves. Hannah was ordered to "publicly acknowledge her sin and evil" one Lord's Day in 1691 before the church congregation at Braintree, Massachusetts. When the searcher checked the story a little further, he discovered that Hannah and Josiah had been ordered to separate. Why? Because Hannah had been

119

married to Josiah's brother until that brother died leaving her a widow. Therefore, she had once been known as Josiah's sister!

When the Puritan neighbors of Samuel Newton and his wife discovered that she was the widow of his uncle, they told the church fathers. Immediately the marriage (which had lasted several years) was declared void because Samuel's wife was really his aunt. Their two children were called illegitimate even though their parents had been legally married for some time.

Be sure to read every word carefully when you find a missing person's record. Suppose you find that your man was "transported to this country" on board a certain ship. That does not mean he just sailed over. "Transported over" means he was shipped here—or deported. For what reason? One man had stolen library books. Another had stolen a silver shoe buckle. Someone else had stolen a chicken. Of course there were other reasons, too, like arson or embezzlement. Occasionally prisoners in England were given a choice between death and being transported. The word was out that Virginia was "the land of death," however, and many chose death instead. The ones who arrived on these shores were the brave, adventurous type.

You may discover some ancestors who were "bound," or came from the old country as "indentured servants." This was a very respectable way of coming over—on the "travel now, pay later" plan. And did they ever *pay!*

It was the only way for a person to come who wanted to live in the New World and had no money. He would promise his work—and often the work of his wife and children—for a stated number of years to a man who would pay the passage. The man with the money made out doubly well. Often he received more land because he had more adults in his family. He had the promise of help in a new country where he knew life would—at best—be difficult. By the time the indentured servant had paid off his debt and gone his own way, perhaps the master's own children would be old enough to help him.

The bound person took all the risks. If his wife and children died, he not only had to serve his term of years but also theirs, because their passage had been paid for whether they died the first day at sea or not. The master had control over the bound man's children. If the master mistreated a child, the parents could take the matter into court in the hope of stopping the mistreatment, but they rarely did because of the hard feelings such a step would cause. The child could not run away because his family would be forced to serve out his years of "promised" work. He could not even go home to visit his parents if his master chose to have him live somewhere else.

Children were often "bound out" to work when the parents were poor and could not care for him. Orphans especially were bound out. The idea was that the master would feed the child, teach him a trade, and, when the time came for the child to be free (at age twenty-one), send him off with a new suit of clothes to make his way in the world.

Jabez Franklin's mother died when he was only seven. In 1842 his father put him in an orphan home, where they started teaching him to knit stocking legs. In those days stockings were as long as a person's legs and most of them were made in reformatories and orphan homes. Five-year-olds knitted just the straight parts of the stocking, but as soon as a child turned seven, he or she was old enough to do the harder part of turning the heel.

Jabez hated knitting. He was sick so often that finally the director of the orphan home bound him out to a local farmer, Mr. Crossman—who lived up to his name. He was stern and never smiled. But his wife often stood up for Jabez even though she was not supposed to have any opinions of her own. There was never any question of paying Jabez for his day-long work. But, he kept telling himself, if he could only survive for eleven years, he would be rich—with a suit of clothes, a yoke of young oxen, and twenty-five dollars all his own. Many cold nights when his bones ached, Jabez dreamed of the wealth he would have someday. But his dream lasted only two years.

One day when he was twelve, he and Mr. Crossman had a terrible argument over some bean sprouts. There were spaces between the sprouting seeds, Jabez pointed out. Some had come up, but others did not. He had carefully dug out the unsprouted seeds to see whether they had the beginnings of roots and sprouts. Then he carefully planted them again.

"You can't do that!" shouted Mr. Crossman.

"I did it last year and they still grew," Jabez shouted back.

Mr. Crossman was roaring mad by this time and said he would settle the matter with Jabez in the barn.

"Could we let Mrs. Crossman decide the matter?" Jabez suggested.

"No," Mr. Crossman growled. "She seems to think you are always right. I will settle my own way in the barn—at dawn tomorrow morning."

Jabez knew what that meant. That night he crept quietly out of his room in the barn and slipped away.

Soon he was on the towpath of the Erie Canal. A canal boat just going through a lock helped him decide which way to go. When the canal boat continued on its way, Jabez had his first "unbound" job driving two horses toward Albany, New York. Everything he owned was on his back, and in his pocket were three pennies that had been a gift. At Albany, he stowed away on a Hudson River steamboat that took him to New York.

There he searched along the docks for the kind of long, low schooner he had read about in a story called "Buccaneers." He found one, but there was no skull and crossbones flag. Perhaps it was below. While he was standing there admiring the ship, a tall muscular and tanned young man came up from below and asked, "Well, you lubber, what's the matter with you?"

"Sir, are you a pirate? Do you want a boy?" asked Jabez.

Captain Chase, half owner of the boat *Mary Perkins of Cape Cod,* looked at the short, skinny boy on the dock and answered, "Why, yes. Will you join us? We want an experienced sword sharpener."

Jabez sailed four years with Captain Chase, who turned out not to be a pirate after all, but a trader carrying Yankee goods to the West Indies and returning with sugar and molasses. Then he sailed around Cape Horn to San Francisco and Shanghai. Once Jabez bought a dozen young monkeys because he was told "they were orphans" and he planned to give them to his old orphan home. But they all jumped ship while at sea. After a life filled with the kinds of adventures that family hunters hope to find in their family history, he settled down to raise his own family in California.

123

No Golden Gate Bridge, no skyscrapers—San Francisco seaport looked like this when Jabez Franklin decided to make his fortune there

You may think you have found just the ancestor to get you into an exclusive club of people whose ancestors came over on the *Mayflower*. That happened to one boy who thought his membership was assured when his most likely suspect was named Thomas Blossom, a preacher among the Puritans who had fled to Leyden, Holland. With only a little more searching, he discovered that Thomas and his wife, Anne, and their children had sailed from Leyden in 1620. Just the year the *Mayflower* sailed! He made out his application for the exclusive club and was about to mail it when a persistent little phrase crept into his mind. It came from a history book back somewhere in the fourth grade—something about the *Mayflower* and the *Speedwell* both sailing at the same time. Only, the *Speedwell* leaked and had to turn back for repairs. Both ships landed in England for the needed repairs, but it seems the *Speedwell* just had too many leaks. The Puritans had to make an agonizing decision. All who could fit into the *Mayflower* sailed for the New World, but the creaky old *Speedwell,* with only eighteen passengers on it by now, returned to Holland. The exclusive-club hopeful sagged in his chair— Thomas Blossom and his family had truly missed the boat!

Have you an ancestor with two wives—at the same time? Try to be tolerant. The trip to the New World was not comparable to any other experience most men had ever had. Until he made the journey, a man had no idea what it could be like. Some ships made fairly comfortable voyages—meaning that most of the people arrived alive. Others ran into terrible storms. On some, diseases broke out killing many of the passengers. Still other ships wallowed in calms, hardly moving ten feet a day, while the water and food slowly ran out. A man thought twice about suggesting that his wife and young ones take the next boat over. Yet he had no money to go back. And the prospects of finding much money over here were not so good as he had allowed himself to believe back in the old country. Sometimes it was the wife who stubbornly refused to follow her husband. At any rate, with an ocean between the two people, many a man took another wife in the New World to start out his new life with him.

Are some of your people not legally married? Besides the reason just explained above, there were other reasons why such a thing could happen. Many people lived where the preacher visited about once a year. Occasionally a traveling preacher, on the lookout for ways to save souls, got everyone together and married them all at the same time, just so as not to miss anyone. After the Civil War, the occupying general of some Southern towns refused permission to marry for anyone not willing to give an oath of allegiance first. People who still had hopes that the South would rise again were not about to give such an oath.

One family searcher was embarrassed to find that so many of her ancestors could not read or write. There was little time for schooling among the children of early pioneers. Most people were farmers or were skilled at some trade like blacksmithing, carpentry, keeping a store. Even people who had been gentlemen and gentlewomen in the old country soon learned that this new world could not support the occupation of "gentleman," so they had to roll up their sleeves and work, too. Children were thought of only as "small adults." Their jobs were sometimes as hard as the jobs of the "big adults." Besides, schools cost money. Many states did have free schools before 1876, but in order for children to go to them free, parents had to sign an oath saying they were paupers and could not afford to pay. At that time, being uneducated was no disgrace. Saying you were a pauper was!

Did you have an ancestor who was hanged? Life was cheap in the old days and many times the laws did not fit the crimes. Don't condemn your criminal without knowing all the circumstances. A young man in his teens might spend months in a city prison just because he ran out of money in a strange town where he knew no one. A man who took a person's life was called a murderer whether he had done it on purpose or by accident. Some colonies in North America were settled by people who were considered criminals. Some of them really were undesirables, but many others were people whose only crime was not being able to pay their debts. Find out the reason for your person's social problem. Court records are not very hard to examine if you know when and where the trial took place.

Johnny Weber was ninety-four years old in 1970. Somewhere, he had seventeen brothers and sisters—if any were still living. He had spent forty-four years in the Ohio State Penitentiary and had very little to look forward to, when someone suggested that he search for his family. Soon Johnny was getting letters and cards and gifts from all over the world. A doctor in Austria sent him his family tree and told him that now he, Johnny, had been found, the doctor had been able to fill in 117 missing family members!

Another searcher discovered a relative who had killed himself with an overdose of opium. Was there an addict in the family? She did not know whether to keep on learning more about him or lose him conveniently. Why had he killed himself? Joseph Fish had once been the editor of a political newspaper. When the candidate he was backing for president was defeated, Joseph lost everything he had. Then he remembered the advertisement his paper had carried in the fall of 1848—about gold in California. He decided that was the solution to all his problems at once.

Joseph's descendant has some of the letters he wrote on his way to becoming a "millionaire." "Our loads are now about 1100 pounds to each wagon," he says, writing on the banks of the Kansas River in May. "With this light load we hope to go through at a lively rate and rip right through the gullies which are very numerous over the prairies. A few miles from here we met a small party just from the gold region on their way home. I judge there were about 15 or 20 men with pack mules and one four-mule wagon. . . . They were pushing along at a rapid rate. This party was loaded with the gold dust. They informed us that some of them had collected at the rate of $500 a day. The meeting with this party had an enlivening effect upon our party and some seemed to think that we had already arrived at the Eldorado."

But neither Joseph nor any of his friends ever found the gold they dreamed of. Instead, his friends died of fevers and drownings. Three years later, Joseph gave up his hunt for gold, but by now he had all the symptoms of tuberculosis. He took more and more of the medicines he could find. Today doctors know those medicines were full of opium and morphine. He was a drug addict—and so was every other man, woman, and infant who took the same medicines.

"My family must be a bunch of coldhearted monsters," wailed one family hunter. She had found a notation in a family diary after the death of the baby of the family. It said,

Blest are they who have a dear one dead because they have a dear companionship that will never change.

Death was so common just a hundred years ago that few people were naïve enough to believe they could raise an entire family of children without losing some little ones. There were no antibiotics to cool fevers, no knowledge of germs, vitamins, or blood types. Many people died of typhoid fever because they thought clear water was clean water. And because dying was so common, they had to find the strength to live with the disasters that happened. Small children were taught songs about death from first grade on. And when a child died, people comforted the mother by saying, "The blossoms fall from the tree in the spring, but life still goes on."

You do know that someone had to fight on the "other" side in the Revolutionary War, don't you? Don't bury your person again just because you find

You may have had ancestors on both sides in the Revolutionary War

a notation like this about him:

> A_____ McLean was imprisoned by request of the Honorable John Hancock, Esq., President of Congress, with the following notice: Take charge of a certain Mr. McLean as a person Inimical to the Liberties of America and have him safely kept. He was committed to the committee of Safety, Philadelphia, 15 June 1776, with orders to keep him safely until the Congress shall take order concerning him.

Parade your Loyalist ancestor—just look whose attention he attracted! John Hancock's, no less. Besides, it was only June 15. He might have changed his mind by July 4!

Are eloping ancestors your problem? One descendant found that a rich young girl in her family had fallen in love with a free black man. To this day many of their descendants live in one New Jersey town— half of them as white people and half as blacks. Another discovered an energetic old man who had already outlived two wives, when his daughters objected to his taking a third.

At eighty-one, Joshua could still walk without a cane and could step lively across a plank laid over a brook, his cane tucked under his arm. Why shouldn't he marry the widow Hannah? he shouted.

"Because she is the age of your daughters!" his children shouted back.

Joshua's children did everything they could to prevent his marriage to a child bride of forty-five. But Joshua knew his children and their habits better than they thought. He told Hannah to be in the meadow near the church early one morning. He thrust a piece of paper into the hands of the preacher. On it was his own version of a speedy marriage ceremony.

"Here, read that quick!" he commanded. "If you don't, I will."

The minister read it as fast as he could and when the children arrived for church soon after, they found Papa and his new wife there to greet them.

The family hunter cannot forget that he is dealing with human beings and not just names on a page. Your family will surprise you dozens of times. Truth, you will find, proves to be stranger than fiction—especially in genealogy.

7

So You Always Hated History!

Peeople who are trying to find their roots are not history addicts at first. But they cannot help running into history—because that is where their roots go. In order to follow, you may have to trade your sneakers for the high-top shoes your ancestor wore and walk right in his footsteps.

David and Louisa Lindenman were married after the Civil War ended. Having spent three years serving his country, David was more than happy to be just a farmer. But their children arrived in more quantity than the crops. Within six years, there were five children. Then the doctor ordered a change of climate because he feared for Louisa's life.

Just that very month, the Homestead Act provided special benefits for Union veterans. In accordance with the provisions of that act David went to the new territory, Kansas, to look over the 160 acres that

HOMESTEAD.

Land Office at *Brownville Neb*
January 20ᵃ 1868.

CERTIFICATE,
No. 1

APPLICATION,
No. 1

It is hereby certified, *That pursuant to the provisions of the act of Congress, approved May 20, 1862, entitled "An act to secure homesteads to actual settlers on the public domain,"* *Daniel Truman* has made payment in full for *E½ of NW¼ & W½ of NW¼ & SW¼ of NE¼* of Section *Twenty six (26)* in Township *four (4) N.* of Range *five (5) E* containing *160* acres.

Now, therefore, be it known, *That on presentation of this Certificate to the* COMMISSIONER OF THE GENERAL LAND OFFICE, *the said Daniel Truman shall be entitled to a Patent for the Tract of Land above described.*

Henry M. Atkinson *Register.*

This is the certificate of the man who was first in line one bitter cold day in 1868 in Nebraska

would be his, provided he lived on that land with his family and cultivated it for five years. Soon he was back in Illinois, grinning and laughing and helping his wife to pack their belongings into a covered wagon for the trip to Kansas—and their new farm. To a student in a history class, the Homestead Act may be just another dull date to remember. But to the descendants of David and Louisa, the June 1872 provision for Union veterans meant new life for their ancestors. Kansas was the birthplace of little Emma Kittie Irene, who was the only survivor of Louisa's triplets born a few years later and who bears all three of the babies' names by herself.

Emma Kittie Irene wrote this about her homestead:

> My father, with the help of two young nephews, dug back into a hill side and made what was called a dugout on his new farm. I don't know the dimensions but it was one large room, big enough to cook, eat, live, and sleep in quite comfortably. The walls were built up of stone, plastered and white washed and a fresh coat of white wash was applied every year. But for several years the floor was just dirt, well packed. There was space dug out on north and south sides for four panes and a full size window and door in the east end.

Living in a sod house had its drawbacks, though, as Emma Kittie Irene discovered one night when she had been told to go to bed.

> I stood and watched what I thought was a snake wriggling in the wall. I had just the light that shone in from our living room so was not sure and didn't want to be laughed at if I was mistaken. But when my father scolded me for not going in to bed, I said, "I think there is a snake here in the wall," so he came in and killed it. It was only about a foot long, what was called a little house snake.

History becomes today's story, instead of something old, when you live through it with your ancestors. Especially surprising is the drama of the small historic moments that history books pass through so quickly.

"From the halls of Montezuma to the shores of Tripoli" are the beginning words of the U.S. Marine hymn. Many history books tell about Montezuma and

National Archives

The gun has just gone off and the great Oklahoma land rush is on near Orlando, September 16, 1893

One week later, the lucky landholders are waiting in line to file their claims. Could one of these men be your ancestor?

National Archives

of the golden treasures of ancient Mexico. But who knows much about the shores of Tripoli?

"The U.S. government ended the power of the Barbary pirates," says an elementary school history book. To the student who is happy when the recess bell rings, that ends another history chapter. But to Jonathon Cowdery, a Navy surgeon imprisoned by the cruel Pasha of Tripoli, history did not move so fast.

For two years the U.S. Government had been blackmailed into paying the rulers of Tunis, Tripoli, Algiers, and Morocco, so that African pirates would not rob American ships. But in spite of the two million dollars paid, American ships were still being pillaged. The situation worsened when the Pasha of Tripoli, furious because the ruler of Algiers was getting more money than he was, declared war on the United States. Immediately, American ships were sent to blockade the port of Tripoli. One ship was the frigate *Philadelphia,* and on it was Dr. Jonathon Cowdery.

One of the pirate ships soon teased the captain of the *Philadelphia* into a chase that ended when the frigate struck a rock offshore. After a fierce day of fighting, the captain and three hundred men were taken prisoner on October 31, 1803. The officers were imprisoned, but the seamen were forced to do slave labor.

The prisoners were certain they would be rescued. Help would come soon. But months went by. Then on the night of February 16, 1804, two ships were seen offshore. Was rescue on the way? The prisoners did not know whether to hope their government would save them or to hope it would choose to fight the pirates instead. That night Stephen Decatur and his marines boarded the frigate *Philadelphia,* which the pirates had refloated for themselves. They set the frigate on fire and escaped back to their own ships. This was in the early days of the U.S. Marine Corps, and the terrorist pirates now had some idea what sort of enemy they had declared war on.

More months went by. In August, the Americans fiercely attacked Tripoli.

"On August 5," Dr. Cowdery wrote in his journal, "the American squadron anchored off Tripoli. I was ordered to dress a wound of a Mamuluke who had his hand shattered by the bursting of a blunderbuss. I amputated all his fingers but one, with a dull knife, and dressed them in a bungling manner, in hopes of losing my credit as a surgeon in this part of the country, for I expected to have my hands full of wounded Turks, in consequence of the exploits of my brave countrymen."

The thirteenth of August, the Pasha demanded a million dollars for the release of his captives as well as the release of several pirate prisoners. Every so often the American prisoners would be treated more cruelly so that the U.S. Government would hurry up and pay the ransom. But by April, the Pasha was wearing a more worried look. He sent for Dr. Cowdery and questioned him.

"April 19. The Bashaw [Pasha] interrogated me concerning my country and force. He asked me how many Marines the U.S. kept in pay. My answer, for good reasons, was 10,000. How many troops? he asked. Eighty thousand said I are in readiness to march and defend the country at any moment and nearly one million of militia are also ready to fight for the rights and for their countrymen. At this his highness assumed a very serious look and I retired to my room."

Slowly the captured prisoners were able to piece

together what was worrying the Pasha. He had been on the throne for eleven years—after first killing his elder brother and exiling another brother. Now it appeared that the U.S. Marines had struck a bargain with the exiled brother, one that would work better than paying the ransom demands. The brother needed fighting men to regain his throne. And the United States needed a new Pasha in power. So they got together. As the army marched toward Tripoli with the new Pasha in the rear, the prisoners noticed many signs that the affair was finally coming to a head. The old Pasha was plainly sorry now that he had not settled for money when he had had the chance.

Finally on May 26, three frigates appeared offshore. At about 11:00 A.M., the smallest came near shore and hoisted banners of peace. A week later, the terms were agreed upon and the prisoners were free to go at last. Their piece of history lasted almost twenty months, though it merited only a sentence in one school textbook.

Every genealogist hopes to find at least one hero. The most likely place for a full-fledged one is during a war. Since the records of World War I and World War II servicemen, Korean and Vietnam veterans, are still considered confidential (for at least seventy-five years after each event), the searcher must get stories of those wars by questioning relatives. Be sure to do it now while the stories are still remembered by someone who witnessed them.

For other wars, look through your list of likely candidates and see whether any of your people could have been in the regular army, navy, marines, or revenue cutter service (today's Coast Guard), or in volunteer units during these dates:

Revolutionary War (1775–1783)
Indian wars (between 1817 and 1898)
War of 1812 (1812–1815)
Mexican War (1846–1848)
Civil War (1861–1865)
Spanish-American War (1898)
Puerto Rico Regiment of Volunteers (1899–1901)
Philippine Insurrection (1899–1903)

Next, find out what outfit your person was with. Was he one of the volunteers or was he in the militia? The militiamen were comparable to today's National Guard. They were organized within the state and therefore all their records are still found in the state record offices. Records of men or women in the Continental Army, U.S. Army, U.S. Navy, U.S. Marines, and the Army, Navy, and Marines of the Confederate States are preserved in the National Archives in Washington, D.C.

"My grandfather fought in one of the Indian wars but I don't know just where or when," says Emma Kittie Irene's journal. On such slim evidence, one of her descendants searched through the National Archives records to find he had taken part in the Sac and Fox Indian War of 1831, one of the times the government did not stand by its treaty with the Indians. You will find many of your people with the tantalizing line after their names: "fought in the Revolution," or "two years in the Civil War." Then you have to find out what they did and where.

There are two main kinds of records. One is the person's service record, but often not much information for the family searcher is in it. The other is the record of veterans benefits—which has quite a bit of genealogical information. Since the government

History books make Civil War soldiers sound like grim warriors.
Your ancestor might have been a fun-loving reluctant recruit

could not afford to pay its troops well, it paid pensions
to the men who were disabled or to the wives of men
who were killed and it also gave bounty land in payment. In order to receive those veterans benefits, your
person (or his wife) had to file applications, which
included much of the information you want to have
about them. Fortunately these records are well indexed.

There is always the chance, however, that your
person was in the war and missed the whole thing!
That is what happened to William Mefford.

William could hardly wait for his turn to come. His
father and four brothers were already fighting. But

his family talked him into waiting until he was twenty-one. Finally in December 1781 he enlisted in the Maryland militia, but instead of fighting in glorious battles, he was assigned to guard British prisoners. In March he decided to try fighting the war on the seas. He went to Philadelphia and signed on board a ship—which turned out to be a big mistake in many ways.

No sooner was William over his first bout of seasickness than a British frigate bore down on the little ship he had chosen and imprisoned the whole crew. William and the others were shipped all over the West Indies, finally landing on a prison ship off the coast of Antigua. There he literally sweated out the rest of the war until he was exchanged a year later and was free to return. On the way home, he learned for the first time that Cornwallis had surrendered at Yorktown four months earlier.

But the war might not be over yet—no treaty had been signed. The day after he finally landed in Maryland, William enlisted aboard a privateer schooner. One month later, peace was declared and the war was ended. Years later, when William applied for a serviceman's pension, he discovered that the ships he had served on were privately owned and were not part of the real navy at all. He was not even entitled to call himself a war hero. However, even though the National Archives had no service records for William Mefford, there were records showing that he had applied for a pension.

If your person's trail leads to anything having to do with the federal (not state) government, then you may find his records filed away in the National Archives. You do not have to take the next plane to Washington, D.C., to see them, however. You can send for information from them by mail:

Write for the form GSA—6751, Order for Copies of Veterans Records:

> General Services Administration
> National Archives
> Washington, D.C. 20408

The form, which is free, is illustrated here so you can see what sort of information you should have in order to fill out your request. The same form is used for a veteran of any war—but don't ask about wars that happened before 1776 when the United States was not yet a nation. While you are asking, request a few extra forms.

For about a dollar, you can receive up to ten pages from the file of any veteran. If your soldier's file contains more than ten pages, the archivist will try to select the best ten and the return answer will indicate that there are more pages on file. Then you ask how much it would cost you for copies of all the pages in his file. In case you have to buy very many, a "negative" copy (white on black) is cheaper than a "positive." At least a month, maybe two, will pass before you receive the reply from the Archives, because they are swamped with applications like yours.

What you get back is your person's record in *one* military organization. If you happen to know that he transferred to another group, fill out another form to find his record there. Some records are not included. If you know he was court-martialed, send another GSA form with "Send All Court-Martial Records" written across the top. If you know he was wounded, send another form with "Send Complete Medical Records" written across the top.

A book that will tell you exactly what records are

GENERAL SERVICES ADMINISTRATION

ORDER FOR COPIES—VETERANS RECORDS
(See reverse for explanation)

DATE RECEIVED

REQUIRED MINIMUM IDENTIFICATION OF VETERAN

| 1. NAME OF VETERAN *(Last name, first, middle)* | 2. WAR IN WHICH OR DATES BETWEEN WHICH HE SERVED | 3. IF SERVICE WAS CIVIL WAR ☐ UNION ☐ CONFEDERATE |

4. CHECK RECORD DESIRED

☐ PENSION   ☐ BOUNTY LAND WARRANT APPLICATION *(Service before 1856 only)*   ☐ MILITARY

5. STATE FROM WHICH HE SERVED

PLEASE PROVIDE THE FOLLOWING INFORMATION IF KNOWN

6. UNIT IN WHICH HE SERVED *(Name of regiment or number, company, etc., or name of ship)*

7. BRANCH IN WHICH HE SERVED
☐ INFANTRY ☐ CAVALRY ☐ ARTILLERY ☐ NAVY ☐ OTHER *(Specify)*

8. KIND OF SERVICE
☐ VOLUNTEERS ☐ REGULARS

9. PENSION OR BOUNTY LAND FILE NUMBER

10. DATE OF BIRTH

11. PLACE OF BIRTH

12. NAME OF WIDOW OR OTHER CLAIMANT

13. DATE OF DEATH

14. PLACE OF DEATH

15. IF VETERAN LIVED IN A HOME FOR SOLDIERS, ENTER LOCATION *(City and State)*

16. PLACE(S) WHERE VETERAN LIVED AFTER SERVICE

17. INDICATE HERE THE NUMBER OF ADDITIONAL COPIES OF THIS FORM (GSA FORM 6751) DESIRED

INSTRUCTIONS

PRINT OR TYPE YOUR NAME AND ADDRESS (including ZIP Code) WITHIN THE DOTS BELOW

Submit a separate form for each veteran. Do not send payment with your order. You will be billed $2.00 for each file reproduced. Mail your order to:

Military Service Records (NNCC)
National Archives (GSA)
Washington, DC 20408

DO NOT WRITE IN THIS AREA
REPLY

RECORD(S) ENCLOSED ☐ PENSION ☐ BOUNTY LAND ☐ MILITARY

RECORD(S) NOT FOUND ☐ PENSION ☐ BOUNTY LAND ☐ MILITARY

☐ ENCLOSED ARE COPIES FROM _____ FILES. YOU ARE BEING BILLED $2.00 FOR EACH FILE REPRODUCED.   ☐ SEE ATTACHED BILL.

☐ WE FOUND _____ PENSION OR BOUNTY LAND FILES AND _____ MILITARY SERVICE FILES FOR VETERANS OF THE SAME NAME (OR SIMILAR VARIATIONS). YOU MAY ORDER COPIES BY RETURNING THE ENCLOSED MARKED FORMS.

☐ WHEN WE ARE UNABLE TO FIND A RECORD FOR A VETERAN, THIS DOES NOT NECESSARILY MEAN THAT HE DID NOT SERVE. YOU MAY BE ABLE TO OBTAIN MORE INFORMATION ABOUT HIM FROM THE STATE ARCHIVES.

☐ SEE ATTACHED FORMS/LEAFLETS.   ☐ SEE REVERSE.

☐ PLEASE COMPLETE BLOCKS 1 *(give full name)*, 2, AND 5 AND RESUBMIT.

☐ A REFUND OF $ _____ ☐ WILL BE SENT BY THE TREASURY DEPARTMENT. ☐ IS ENCLOSED.   REFUND AUTHORIZATION

SEARCHER   FILE DESIGNATION

DATE

CASHIER

GSA FORM **6751** (REV. 9-74)

This is the form you will send to the National Archives for a copy of your own soldier-hero's record in the National Archives can be purchased for under two dollars from a genealogical supply house (see list at the back of this book) or from the Archives. It is *Guide to Genealogical Records in the National Archives,* by Meredith B. Colket and Frank E. Bridgers.

If you live near Washington, D.C., or are planning a trip there on vacation, you can visit the Genealogy Section of the Archives, provided you are over sixteen. You must be accompanied by an adult if you are under sixteen. Be sure you have a driver's license or something for identification, because you must first get a permit to use the facilities. Take with you the information you have about the relative you want to find and go early in the morning if you want to ask to see his records. Applications to see records that are turned in late in the day will not be taken care of until the next morning. However, you will have to wait only about an hour instead of a month or so to "see" your war hero. And you can have the copies made that you want to take home with you.

Since only thirteen of the twenty-two British colonies signed the Declaration of Independence, many ancestors may have stayed pro-British. Some of them were Tories and some were Loyalists. Tories were not considered too dangerous to the American cause and so their properties were not confiscated when they fled to Canada. However, Loyalists were actually charged with treason and they lost everything when they fled. After 1783, those people who had lost everything because of their loyalty to the British side could make claims and receive some compensation. Their original records are now in the Public Record Office in London, but there are well-indexed microfilmed copies in the Public Archives, Ottawa, Ontario, Canada. In Audit Office No. 12 you can find recorded

The National Archives Building houses the most important
documents of the nation—including your ancestors' war records

the claims for their losses and in Audit Office No. 13 is the evidence of the claimants. No ancestor is ever really "lost." (It is you who are lost.)

A Civil War hero is easier to find if he fought on the Union side, because many records of Confederates were destroyed as the war neared its close. But that does not mean you cannot find a Confederate soldier. Start looking for him in the archives of his own state. Most of the Confederate states tried to pay pensions to their own soldiers, since the Federal Government was in no mood to pay the enemies they had so recently fought. Ask for the military pension records for Confederate soldiers.

Many Southern states have their Confederate veterans records on microfilm and very well indexed. You can locate copies of the Index in most of the Southern state universities and other libraries. A quick check will tell you whether one of your people is listed. Your Union soldier can be found in the lists at the National Archives.

Many books have been written about Civil War soldiers—just as they have been about soldiers of every war. But three sources will be especially helpful for finding your person. Try to find *Tracing Your Civil War Ancestor,* by Bertram H. Groene, in your local library. It is easy to understand and fun to read. The other two sources are indexes: called the OR and the ORN, for short. The OR's real title is *Official Records of the Union and Confederate Armies in the War of the Rebellion* and there are 128 volumes. The ORN has 31 volumes and its real name is *Official Records of the Union and Confederate Navies in the War of the Rebellion.* Although it will be easier to find officers listed in these volumes, there are plenty of enlisted men too. An atlas goes with the books, so you can look up the area where a battle was fought if you find your man surrounded by action. The OR and ORN are found in most large city and state university libraries.

Another kind of hero whose shoes you must also step into, if you are to find him, is your immigrant ancestor. Actually each person has several immigrant ancestors—one for each branch of the family. He was the brave person who dared to sail over an unknown and sometimes vicious ocean, breaking his ties with the Old World. In most cases he, and sometimes his family, came to stay.

To find a person on a ship passenger list, you should know where he came from, what year, and on which ship.

But as with so many family searches, if you knew all that, you would not be reading through passenger lists! Until all the lists have been indexed, passenger lists are not too much help in finding your persons. Actually, some have already been soundexed and so there is hope. But if you can discover, by questioning relatives or friends, the name of the ship and when it arrived and perhaps what port the ship landed in, you will have accomplished something.

Too many family records say something vague like "Came from Scotland in 1733" or "Came from Liverpool." Thousands of people came from Scotland— some of them even stopped off in Ireland for a few years and got married on the way over. As for Liverpool, it was one of the largest ports in England, and half the people who came over from that country sailed from Liverpool. That does not mean they lived in Liverpool. And the shipping lists are arranged all wrong for family hunters: by the quarter year in which the ship landed, the port it landed in, the name of the ship and the name of the captain, and way down at the bottom the name of the passengers you are looking for.

Ship passenger lists do, however, make interesting reading. For instance, Captain Gardner of the *Margaret* carefully described some of the passengers who disembarked in Philadelphia on August 26, 1805, this way:

Name of Passenger	Age	Nativity	Occupation	Description
Joseph Geyger	31	Wurtemberg	farmer	6 ft. 6 in.
Anna "	30			
Johann G. Specht	44			low stature with hump on back
Anna Moss	50	Wurtemberg	gentle-woman	large & black

Passports, which would be a good way to trace modern-day persons, were not required for American citizens until World War I, except for a short time during the Civil War. Still, some people had them. Peter Reist's passport, dated October 15, 1723, stated:

The bearer is departing from here at a place at which no pestilential plague, but thank God, pure air prevails.

In 1730, John Valentine Griesheimer (whose name was mispelled as Valtein Grisimer) and his wife and five children carried a letter certifying that they had been released from serfdom in Prussia and stating that if they ever returned there, they would be serfs again.

From the very beginning, the immigrant ancestors found that things were different in the New World—things they had not expected to be different. And it all had to do with *space*. Because there was plenty of land here, fathers could no longer insist that their daughters marry someone the parents had chosen. Mothers no longer needed to teach daughters to fall in love with an eldest son "because he will inherit all his father's land someday." Every son inherited land.

Almost at once women grew so independent that they began objecting to the "love, honor and obey" kind of marriage ceremony. When they needed money, they were too independent to be servants, but preferred working in factories. Their children ran more freely. They could shout if they wanted to because they no longer lived in crowded quarters. There were so many religions, instead of one state religion, that families divided more quickly.

One of the first acts of an early immigrant was to get some land while it was still plentiful and cheap. This is lucky for family hunters, because land records of various kinds help follow the immigrant's trail. Sometimes the land records tell where the person came from. But people also moved fast once they hitched up mules to a covered wagon, so tracing them requires imagination.

Actually there were some characteristics that make it easier to follow a person. Men did not go very far to find their wives. Even a small mountain was a big obstacle to a man with a wagon. And when men did move out to new lands, they very often took along aunts, uncles, parents, cousins, and everyone they could talk into joining them. This is one reason why family-hunting is never just person-hunting. You never know which member of the family is going to

Perhaps this is one of your missing families—traveling light and moving west as fast as they could in 1886 to find a homestead

supply you with just the clue you need to find the certain person who is related to you. Keep your eyes and ears open.

You can follow an ancestor's footprints better if you have some sort of idea how he traveled. Suppose you have an ancestor who lived in a little town like Huntingdon, Pennsylvania, in 1834. Then suddenly he disappeared. Obviously, he moved—but where?

The answer came quite by accident to a researcher with just this problem. He was reading the diary of a

150

This was the superhighway between Ogden, Utah, and Helena, Montana, in 1871

man named David Jarrett who lived near Philadelphia and who traveled west to Indiana to buy a piece of land. Jarrett's diary not only tells about the town of Huntingdon but mentions that it is on "the canal," one of the main transportation routes to Pittsburgh. It was also on the "National Road," which is Route 22 today. Later, when the researcher discovered that his missing ancestor had moved from Huntingdon, Pennsylvania, to Steubenville, Ohio, he looked again at the diary of David Jarrett. Now he knew exactly what

151

road his ancestor had traveled over, what the land looked like, and even what "motels" (1834 style) lined the roadside—because Jarrett's diary named every one. His diary also gives the twentieth-century traveler an idea of what it was like then to travel a distance that today takes less than an hour.

Left John Hughes tavern the morning of the 6th, passed through Churchtown a distance of three miles, and a very fine country along the Conestoga pike. Came to the turnpike leading from Downingtown to Harrisburg. At this point we eat *(sic)* breakfast and fed our horses at the "Sign of the Blue Ball," and covering a distance of nine miles. We then started for Harrisburg, passing through Swopetown and Hinkletown and crossed the Conestoga Creek, between the two towns, which was about a distance of five miles. From here we went on to the "Sign of the Cross Keys," distance of two miles and watered the horses, and then continued on to the "Sign of the Bell" in Brickerville, a distance of eight miles and fed our horses, we eating a cold bite. We passed the Warwick Church about two miles back of the tavern, and two miles further on we entered on the South Mountain. Covering a distance of seven miles we came to the Cornwall Furnace, belonging to Coleman. We continued through a lime stone valley to the "Sign of the Cross Keys," through Lebanon County and township for a distance of two miles and stopped here to water our horses. We then resumed our journey to the "Sign of the Spread Eagle," where we lodged with a Mr. Carper, in a very fine house with very good entertainment, and the place called Mount Pleasant.

Sometimes you can follow an immigrant ancestor by learning when certain large groups of immigrants arrived. Since they so often clung together, they were easier to trace. For instance, "Scotch Tom" MacFarland arrived in this country in 1729. Later you learn that 6,000 Scotch-Irish who landed in Philadelphia (where "Scotch Tom" landed, according to Grandmother) all traveled together to Harper's Ferry, West Virginia, and that most of them then took the Great Wagon Road down into Virginia.

Or you may be following an ancestor westward. From 1842 to the late 1880's, the "route signs" that marked the road were all natural sights. First there was the "Great American Desert"—that was the prairies. Impatient children were set to work counting off the streams that had to be crossed while morbid travelers counted the many graves beside the trail. The main road ran along the dry, windy "Coast of Nebraska," as they called the Platte River Valley to Fort Kearny. Beyond there, the river forked and the trail plodded on for sixty miles to "California Crossing." Then double teams had to be put on the wagons because of the quicksand. From there, the children strained their eyes to see the "wooded dell" of Ash Hollow, which meant they were nearing the north branch of the Platte. Everyone watched for such highway signs as Court House, Jail Rocks, Chimney Rock, and Mitchell Pass, when they would all have their first view of the Rocky Mountains where the going would really get tough.

A shortcut for California-bound travelers that would take them "southwest to the Salt Lake and thence continuing down to the Bay of San Francisco" was described in just that way in *The Emigrants Guide to Oregon and California*. That was the book read by the leaders of the Donner party who nearly all died when they were stranded by deep snows in the Sierra Mountains. The book had just failed to mention a few other obstacles that might be in the way of a party "continuing down to the Bay of San Francisco." Some of those obstacles were Utah's Wasatch Mountains, over ten thousand feet high, the alkali Salt Lake Desert, the Nevada Desert, and the High Sierras.

There will be many times in searching for your roots that you will have to make guesses—but at least try to make "educated" ones. For example: you are looking for a young man who went to Colorado in 1860 to "get rich quick" and never came back. Should you look for his will or for a marriage license? The chances of finding his will are better because there were twenty men to every woman in Colorado then.

Wherever your ancestors lead, you see a view of history that never came from any history class. Somehow you know how your person felt because a part of you is him or her. Give him a chance to let you know how it was with him. He cannot be judged by the way life is today—he belongs in his own period. Try to walk in his shoes.

8

Getting It
All Together

Finding your roots is important to knowing who you are. It is not usually a life-and-death matter. But for a man named Simas Kudirka it was just that.

On November 23, 1970, a Russian trawler was stopped by a U.S. Coast Guard cutter in the waters near Martha's Vineyard, Massachusetts. While the Russians were being told they were fishing too close to the United States, a man suddenly ran from the trawler and leaped onto the deck of the Coast Guard ship. The man was Kudirka and he begged the captain of the cutter to give him asylum and not return him to the Russians.

By now the Russians were visibly angry and demanded that Kudirka be returned to their ship at once. The Coast Guard crew could see that things would not go well with Kudirka if he were returned to the trawler, but the captain felt he had no other choice. Finally the man was forced to return and, in sight of the American seamen, he was beaten and dragged below decks by the Russians. The Americans had heavy hearts after the episode, but thought there was no way they might have helped. They had understood little of what the man had shouted as he begged for help, but they did remember his name. The next day Simas Kudirka was a name that everyone in the United States saw in the morning newspaper. The captain of the ship was criticized for not helping him, and that was about the end of the matter. Except for one group.

Kudirka had been a Lithuanian—one of the thousands of people whose country had been taken over by the Russians during World War II. His people were no longer allowed to speak their native language and the children were schooled in Communist ways. Only in America could some of the Lithuanian traditions be kept alive. When the Lithuanian-American Community of the U.S.A., Inc., heard about Kudirka and his plea for freedom, they went to the State Department in Washington, D.C., to see what they could do to help him. They did not even know whether he was still alive. But they made waves anyway. The Russians, perhaps surprised that their ordinary seaman had become such a well-known name in America, realized that he had best be kept alive—at least until things cooled down. But the American-Lithuanians made sure things did not cool down.

The Lithuanian-language newspapers printed the story and pressed the U.S. Government for more help. But there was little that could be done. Then suddenly —almost like a miracle—came a clue. Someone thought Kudirka's mother might have been born in the United States—somewhere around New York

City, the person seemed to recall.

A search for her birth records began—a search that could mean life or death to her son now in a Soviet prison camp. Just the hint that Kudirka's mother had been born in this country was not enough. There must be proof. But now there was no stopping the Lithuanians in the free world. At last they traced his mother's birth to Brooklyn, and it was there, in the baptismal records of the Church of St. Mary of the Angels, that the proof was found. Mrs. Kudirka, who had long before gone to Lithuania, had been born a U.S. citizen —and because of that, her son could become a citizen also.

The Russians released Kudirka from prison and gave him and his family exit visas. On November 5, 1974, Simas Kudirka, his wife, son, daughter, and his mother, stepped off a plane at Kennedy Airport into a new life of freedom—thanks to someone's finding his roots!

Now that you have found some of your roots, what can you do about them? Some people are content just to know something about their family, but most will never give up searching for their missing persons. The most important thing now is not to lose the ones you have found.

One old man lost all his roots in a fire. Even though he also lost his belongings, it was losing all those ancestors he had searched out for over twenty-five years that hurt the most. Now his eyes were failing and he could never repeat the work he had done. One of his friends wrote a letter to *The Genealogical Helper*, a magazine whose pages are filled with people sharing their genealogical discoveries. She described the old man's family and asked for anyone with knowledge of any of his people please to write him. They did—and he is gathering his family once more.

The best way to avoid losing everyone again is to share your information with other people in your family. You could make carbon copies of your family tree—but there will be fewer chances for mistakes if you use a copy machine and reproduce your *original* pages. Copy machines can usually be found in libraries, post offices, schools, or, sometimes, your father's office. You should also reproduce the personal record you kept as you went along—showing what information you found in which books or manuscripts. Then send your copies away to each person you intend sharing with—so that all your eggs are not in one basket.

Family lines would disappear more often if it were not for the ancestor hunters who get so excited about finding their own families that they like to help other people. *The Genealogical Helper* and other magazines like it are filled with ideas and offers of help. Fortunately the magazine has an excellent index that lists every single family name mentioned in each issue. You have only to run your finger down the list, find one of your names, and turn to the page to see whether the item is one of your own people.

One lady discovered that her backyard walk was made of tombstones turned upside down! They had evidently been taken years before from a small local cemetery, now buried under a new road. She learned what a valuable back walk she had one day when a lady knocked on her door to ask whether her great-grandfather's name might be on one of the stones. The two women got a shovel and began digging up the walk. Sure enough, there he was, complete with

It gets even harder to find ancestors once the
weeds start growing over their last resting places

birth and death dates—as well as the grave markers of two of his children!

Sometimes people interested in family-hunting find an unusual birth certificate or an antique Bible with family names written inside. One boy visited a ghost town in Nevada and copied the names from the tombstones there. All these people wrote about their finds in *The Genealogical Helper* because they knew that someone, somewhere in the world, was looking for just those people. You can find new "live" relatives, too, in this kind of magazine—by writing to the person (whose address is listed) who is requesting information about one of your relatives.

Another surprise awaits the family searcher who discovers a "family organization." There are thousands of them—made up of people with the same name who get together occasionally for a sort of super-reunion. In between times, many family organizations publish a mimeographed "newspaper" with news of the various family branches. Family organizations have members from all over the world, including the country where the family had its origins. If you cannot find one with your name, why not start one?

If you are one of those who can find no family history with your name on the library shelves, you might try writing one of your own. Don't panic. Family histories come in all sizes—from the fat ones down to a few typewritten sheets enclosed in cardboard binders. The historical library nearest you will be happy to file copies of the work you have done on your family—or even on one particular branch of your family. Having a genuine leather binding does not make your work more valuable—it's what you put inside that counts. Be sure to write how you "documented" or proved your facts. For the information not proved, be sure to write down your source—such as, "Grandma says" or "A note my father jotted on the margin of a book says this."

For many people, the best part about finding their immigrant ancestors is the tracing of those ancestors back to the countries they came from. Many books have been written to help you continue your search overseas. But don't be in too great a hurry to order your passport and stuff your backpack. Much of the search can be done on this side of the ocean. Read a book like Pine's *American Origins* to give you a start. One of the hardest countries to follow a family in is India. One of the simplest is England. And there is hope even for people of an occupied country, since many records were taken to other countries before the occupation.

A side benefit of looking for your roots—either in this country or in another—is visiting unusual places. One young family stopped in an Irish pub one summer day recently and got involved in a discussion about American tourists that was not too flattering.

"They have no idea what our country is really like," argued the Irishman.

The young couple set him straight. Yes, they were tourists, but not typical ones, because they had chosen this particular village to visit for a special reason. And they had just spent the afternoon experiencing the thrill of their lives. The young wife's family had come from this village over a hundred years ago, and, by politely asking questions of villagers, the couple had been directed to an old lady with the same name as the wife's. The old lady was excited about meeting her "American cousins," but more than that, she even knew which little cottage had belonged to the family.

The couple had spent the afternoon there—walking through the grass, touching the wild roses, and smelling the same sea air that her ancestors had loved.

Travel in this country is even simpler, but you may not find many hundred-year-old landmarks. If your family plans a camping trip this summer, you might suggest seeing where your relatives settled in one of the thirteen original colonies or following a wagon trail that led some of your people west. You are guaranteed a detour *off* the interstate routes and into a piece of America that really means something to you. Superhighways are great for getting you there fast

---

You are sure to leave the superhighways on your ancestor-hunting trips, but in 1912 this was the highway

and they have a way of preserving the old countryside you are looking for by keeping the traffic away from it. But you won't understand your missing persons until you get onto the back roads and byways.

Now that you know something about finding people, you will discover other uses for your new skill. Perhaps you have an old Civil War sword with nothing but a name on it. Or you have found an old Colt pistol in an antique store. Such trophies can be bought for a much cheaper price because they have no "history" attached to them. You already know how to begin the search for their "histories" by looking up the military records of their owners. Sometimes people want to discover more about the history of the old house they live in and the lives of the people who built it. Finding the original deed can be hard, but for someone who knows how to use the information available to family hunters, it can be easier.

Some young people become so good at tracing their own families that they discover they can earn money doing someone else's searching. Older people who want to find their families often live hundreds of miles away from the town they need to search in. Get in touch with your local historical society if you find you are good at the job and enjoy family-hunting. A recommendation from your school or town librarian saying that you are capable, enthusiastic, and *accurate* may get you an unusual job for the summer. Naturally, if you live in a large city, you will find more people needing the information you know how to look for. But sometimes even small towns, and especially a county seat, get requests for someone local "who does not cost as much as a trained genealogist."

Genealogy, if you have enjoyed the detective work so far, is a very good occupation. The National Archives gives a course twice a year for people who want to learn the professional ways of family-hunting. The three-week course costs about $250 and is for people who already have a good knowledge of genealogy before they begin. Then their skills are sharpened with courses like "Colonial handwriting—hazards and hints," "Little-known or unexplored records in the National Archives," and "Legal records terminology."

A professional genealogist earns about five dollars an hour, and sometimes more, doing just the kinds of searching you have been learning to do in this book. But a professional has much more know-how than the person who is just hunting his own people. Professionals are employed by libraries and historical societies to help those searchers with their hardest problems. But many more genealogists work for themselves. They advertise their services, and people write to them asking for help or turning over the entire job of family-hunting to the expert.

Many new helps are coming along for the do-it-yourself root hunter. The computer has only begun to show how useful it can be. New indexes are coming out each year as well as new compiled lists, how-to-do-it books, and county and town histories. Since family-hunting has switched from "hunting blue blood and titled ancestors" to finding one's very roots for an entirely different purpose, there will be more emphasis on helping find problem people.

This book does not even pretend to tell you all about how to trace your family. Its purpose is to stir up your imagination enough for you to think, I wonder what my own ancestors were like. And then to show you that this is a kind of do-it-yourself hobby where you can become as expert as you want. No ancestor is hopelessly lost as long as he has a descendant who would like to meet him. Look in the back of the book for suggestions of other books to help you become a more professional root hunter.

Genealogy is like eating peanuts. You may quit for a while, but you will be back. Those roots which you could not trace this year may be easier to trace another year. You have formed a lifelong habit—and it is a rewarding one.

Where to Write for Official Records

There should be an official certificate filed *in the place where the event happened* for every birth and death that occurred in the United States and its outlying areas. Unfortunately, record-keeping has not always been as careful as it is today, so there is a chance you may not be able to find the vital statistics you want for each person. Marriage records, if there are any, are usually found in the same office, but most states did not start keeping those records until more recently.

To get a certified copy of a person's certificate, locate the address of the vital statistics office in the state or area in the following list. Then, either write or go to that office to get a *full copy* (one that contains all the items on the official certificate and the best one for your purposes) or the *short form* (which has less information, but also costs less). If you know the specific cost, send a money order or a certified check—never cash—with your letter. You should never try to get a birth certificate for someone who is still living. Let him send for it himself.

Your letter should give this information:

1. Full name of the person whose certificate you want
2. Sex and race of that person
3. His or her parents' names, including mother's maiden name
4. Exact date of the birth, death, or marriage (month, day, and year)
5. Exact place of birth, death, or marriage (meaning town, county, state, and the hospital if any)

The fee charged usually includes the cost of searching through the records to find your person. However, many offices charge more money for looking if you do not have the exact dates, names, or places. Also, you may run into some trouble getting birth records from certain states, especially if the persons involved could still be living. Since each state began keeping records at a different date, the plus (+) sign after the date indicates when each state started recording.

ALABAMA. Bureau of Vital Statistics, State Department of Public Health, Montgomery, Ala. 36104. Births and deaths 1908+. Marriages August 1936+. Marriage records can also be found in the probate court of each county. MOBILE records: births 1871+, deaths 1820+, Mobile County Board of Health, P.O. Box 4533, Mobile, Ala. 36604. Marriages, Probate Court Office, County Courthouse, Mobile, Ala. 36604.

ALASKA. Bureau of Vital Statistics, State Department of Health and Welfare, State Office Building, Juneau, Alaska 99801. Records 1913+.

AMERICAN SAMOA. Registrar of Vital Statistics, Government of American Samoa, Pago Pago, American Samoa 96920. Births, deaths, marriages 1900+.

ARIZONA. Bureau of Vital Statistics, State Board of Health, Phoenix, Ariz. 85007. Births, deaths, marriages 1909+.

ARKANSAS. Bureau of Vital Statistics, State Department of Health, 4815 W. Markham Street, Little Rock, Ark. 72201. Births and deaths 1914+, marriages 1917+.

CALIFORNIA. Bureau of Vital Statistics and Data Processing, State Department of Public Health, 631 J Street, Sacramento, Calif. 95814. Births and deaths 1905+. Marriage records are kept by County Clerks, July 1905+. OAKLAND and ALAMEDA records: Alameda County Health Department, 499 5th Street, Oakland, Calif. 94607. BERKELEY records: Berkeley City Health Department, Bureau of Vital Statistics, 2121 McKinley Avenue, Berkeley, Calif. 94703. LONG BEACH records: Vital Statistics Office, Long Beach City Health Department, P.O. Box 6157, Long Beach, Calif. 90806. LOS ANGELES records: Los Angeles County Health Department, Room 900, 220 N. Broadway, Los Angeles, Calif. 90012. PASADENA records: Pasadena City Health Department, Division of Vital Statistics, 100 N. Garfield Avenue, Pasadena, Calif. 91109. SAN FRANCISCO records: births 1905+, deaths 1865+, San Francisco Department of Public Health, 101 Grove Street, San Francisco, Calif. 94102.

CANAL ZONE. Registrar of Vital Statistics, Canal Zone Government, Health Director's Office, Box M, Balboa Heights, C.Z. Births and deaths 1905+.

COLORADO. Records and Statistics Section, State Department of Health, 4210 E. 11th Avenue, Denver, Colo. 80220. Births and deaths 1910+. Some records date back to 1860's. Marriages 1904 to 1940 and 1968+.

CONNECTICUT. Public Health Statistics Section, State Department of Health, 79 Elm Street, Hartford, Conn. 06115. Births and deaths 1897+. Birth records strictly confidential. Birth, death, and marriage records are also filed with each Town Clerk.

DELAWARE. Bureau of Vital Statistics, State Board of Health, P.O. Box 637, Dover, Del. 19901. Births and deaths 1860+, marriages 1847+. For earlier records, check with Clerk of the Peace in each county.

DISTRICT OF COLUMBIA. D.C. Department of Public Health, Vital Records Division, 300 Indiana Avenue,

N.W., Washington, D.C. 20001. Births 1871+, deaths 1855 +. Marriages 1811+, Marriage License Bureau, U.S. District Court, Washington, D.C. No death records filed during Civil War.

FLORIDA. Bureau of Vital Statistics, State Department of Health, P.O. Box 210, Jacksonville, Fla. 32201. Births 1865 +, deaths 1877+, marriages 1927+. Write to County Judge in each county for marriage records.

GEORGIA. Vital Records Service, State Department of Public Health, 47 Trinity Avenue, S.W., Atlanta, Ga. 30334. Births and deaths 1919+. For records before 1919 in Atlanta or Savannah, write County Health Department in place where event occurred. Marriage records kept since June 9, 1952.

GUAM. Office of Vital and Health Statistics, Department of Public Health and Social Services, Government of Guam, P.O. Box 2816, Agana, Guam 96910. Births and deaths October 26, 1901+, marriages 1899+.

HAWAII. State Department of Health, Research and Statistics Office, P.O. Box 3378, Honolulu, Hawaii 96801. Births 1850+, deaths 1861+, marriages 1849+.

IDAHO. State Department of Health, Bureau of Vital Statistics, Boise, Idaho 83707. Births, deaths, marriages: 1911+. Marriage records are in custody of County Recorder for each county.

ILLINOIS. Department of Public Health, Bureau of Vital Records, 525 W. Jefferson Street, Springfield, Ill. 62706. Births and deaths 1916+. Marriage records are in custody of each County Clerk from date of county's organization. CHICAGO records: 1955+, Chicago Board of Health, Room CL, 111 Civic Center, 50 W. Washington St., Chicago, Ill. 60602. PEORIA records: births 1878+, deaths 1872+, Peoria City Health Department, 2116 N. Sheridan Road, Peoria, Ill. 61604.

INDIANA. Division of Vital Records, State Board of Health, 1330 W. Michigan Street, Indianapolis, Ind. 46206. Births October 1907+, deaths 1900+, marriages 1958+. For birth and death records from 1882 to 1908, write to County Clerk of each county, or check with the State Library, Indianapolis. Early marriage records are in custody of each County Clerk from date of organization of county. Address of State Library is 126 N. Senate Avenue, Indianapolis, Ind. 46204. GARY records: 1908+, Gary City Board of Health, Vital Records Department, 1429 Virginia Street, Gary, Ind. 46407. Lake County Clerk has records from 1882 to 1908.

IOWA. Division of Records and Statistics, State Department of Health, Des Moines, Iowa 50319. Births 1880+, deaths 1896+, marriages 1916+. Although records exist for all three since 1880, searches will be made only for the periods since the dates given above. Marriage records are in probate court for each county and date back to the organization of the county.

KANSAS. State Department of Health, Division of Vital Statistics, Records Section, Topeka, Kans. 66612. Births and deaths 1911+, marriages 1913+. For births and deaths after 1892 in Kansas City, write City Clerk, City Hall, 6th and Ann, Kansas City, Kans. 66101.

KENTUCKY. Office of Vital Statistics, State Department of Health, 275 E. Main Street, Frankfort, Ky. 40601. Births and deaths 1911+, marriages 1958+. Earlier marriages, dating from organization of county, can be found with each County Clerk.

LOUISIANA. Division of Public Health Statistics, State Department of Health, P.O. Box 60630, New Orleans, La. 70160. Births and deaths 1914+ for the entire state except the city of New Orleans. Marriage records are in local parishes (counties) in custody of Clerk of Court. NEW ORLEANS records: births 1790+, deaths 1804+, marriages 1831+, Bureau of Vital Statistics, New Orleans

City Health Department, 1 WO 3 City Hall, Civic Center, New Orleans, La. 70112.

MAINE. Office of Vital Statistics, State Department of Health and Welfare, State House, Augusta, Maine 04330. Births, deaths, marriages: 1892+. Earlier records may be found in files of Town Clerk of town where event occurred.

MARYLAND. Division of Vital Records, State Department of Health, State Office Building, 301 West Preston Street, Baltimore, Md. 21201. Births and deaths 1898+, marriages June 1951+, for the entire state except the city of Baltimore. Very early marriage records are at the Hall of Records, Annapolis, Md. BALTIMORE records: births and deaths 1875+, Baltimore City Health Department, Bureau of Vital Records, Municipal Office Building, Baltimore, Md. 21202.

MASSACHUSETTS. Office of the Secretary of State, Division of Vital Statistics, 272 State House, Boston, Mass. 02133. Births, deaths, marriages, 1841+, for the entire state except the city of Boston. Earlier records can be found in files of City or Town Clerk where event occurred. BOSTON records: for records since 1639, write City Registrar, Registry Division, Health Department, Room 705, City Hall Annex, Boston, Mass. 02133.

MICHIGAN. Vital Records Section, Michigan Department of Health, 3500 N. Logan Street, Lansing, Mich. 48914. Births and deaths 1867+, marriages 1868+. DETROIT records: births 1893+, deaths 1897+, City Health Department.

MINNESOTA. Section of Vital Statistics, State Department of Health, 350 State Office Building, St. Paul, Minn. 55101. Births and deaths 1900+. Marriage records are in custody of Clerk of the District Court in each county. Address inquiries to Section of Vital Statistics, State Department of Health, 717 Delaware Street, S.E., Minneapolis, Minn. 55440.

MISSISSIPPI. State Board of Health, Vital Records Registration, P.O. Box 1700, Jackson, Miss. 39205. Births and deaths 1912+. Marriage records 1926+ are in custody of Clerk of the Circuit Court in each county. Many marriage records back to 1826+ are at the Department of Archives and History, Jackson, Miss.

MISSOURI. Vital Records, Division of Health, State Department of Public Health and Welfare, Jefferson City, Mo. 65101. Births and deaths 1910+. Marriage records are in custody of Recorder of Deeds in each county and many date back to county organization. KANSAS CITY records: Kansas City Health Department, 10th Floor, City Hall, Kansas City, Mo. 64106. For marriage records, write Jackson County Recorder of Deeds. ST. LOUIS records: births 1870+, deaths 1850+, St. Louis Department of Health, Bureau of Vital Statistics, Room 10, Municipal Courts Building, 1320 Market Street, St. Louis, Mo. 63103.

MONTANA. Division of Records and Statistics, State Department of Health, Helena, Mont. 59601. Births and deaths 1907+, marriages 1943+. Earlier marriage records, dating from organization of county, are in custody of Clerk of Court of each county.

NEBRASKA. Bureau of Vital Statistics, State Department of Health, Box 94757, Lincoln, Nebr. 68509. Births and deaths 1904+, marriages 1909+. Earlier marriage records are in custody of County Judge in each county. OMAHA records: Omaha-Douglas County Health Department, Division of Vital Statistics, 1602 S. 50th Street, Omaha, Nebr. 68106.

NEVADA. Department of Health, Welfare, and Rehabilitation, Division of Health, Section of Vital Statistics, Carson City, Nev. 89701. Births and deaths July 1911+, marriages 1968+. Earlier marriage records are in custody of County Recorder of each county.

NEW HAMPSHIRE. State Department of Health and Welfare, Bureau of Vital Statistics, 61 S. Spring Street, Concord, N.H. 03301. Births, deaths, marriages: 1640+. Town Clerk of each town also has these vital statistics.

NEW JERSEY. State Department of Health, Bureau of Vital Statistics, P.O. Box 1540, Trenton, N.J. 08625. Births, deaths, marriages: 1878+. The records from May 1848 through May 1878 are in the Archives and History Bureau, State Library Division, Trenton, N.J. Some records of 1665 to 1880 are in Vol. 22, New Jersey Archives, Series 1. CAMDEN records 1924+: Camden City Department of Health, Bureau of Vital Statistics, Room 103, City Hall, Camden, N.J. 08101. ELIZABETH records 1848+: Elizabeth City Department of Health, Bureau of Vital Statistics, City Hall, Elizabeth, N.J. 07201. NEWARK records 1850+: Newark City Division of Health, Bureau of Vital Statistics, City Hall, Newark, N.J. 07102. PATERSON records 1902+ and 1910+: Paterson City Board of Health, 25 Mill Street, Paterson, N.J. 07501.

NEW MEXICO. State Department of Health and Social Services, P.O. Box 2348, Santa Fe, N. Mex. 87501. Births and deaths 1920+. Write County Clerk of each county for marriage records.

NEW YORK. Bureau of Vital Records, State Department of Health, 84 Holland Avenue, Albany, N.Y. 12208. Births, deaths, marriages, 1880+, except for New York City, Albany, Buffalo, and Yonkers. NEW YORK CITY: see the individual boroughs of *Bronx, Brooklyn, Manhattan, Queens,* and *Richmond. Bronx:* Bronx District Health Center, 1826 Arthur Avenue, Bronx, N.Y. 10457. *Brooklyn:* records from 1847 to 1865, County Clerk, Kings County, Historical Division, 360 Adams Street, Brooklyn, N.Y. 11201; records since 1866, Bureau of Records and Statistics, Department of Health of New York City, 295 Flatbush Avenue Ext., Brooklyn, N.Y. 11201. *Manhattan:* Manhattan District Health Center, 125 Worth Street, New York City, N.Y. 10013. Records from 1847 to 1865 are at Municipal Archives and Records Retention Center of New York Public Library, 238 William Street, New York City, N.Y. 10038. *Queens:* Queens District Health Center,

90–37 Parsons Boulevard, Jamaica, N.Y. 11432. Records before 1898 are in Albany. Marriage records are in custody of City Clerk, 88–11 Sutphin Boulevard, Jamaica, N.Y. 11435. *Richmond:* Richmond District Health Center, 55–61 Stuyvesant Place, St. George, Staten Island, N.Y. 10301. Records before 1898 are in Albany. ALBANY records 1870+: Albany City Health Department, Registrar of Vital Statistics, City Hall, Albany, N.Y. 12207. BUFFALO records: Buffalo City Health Department, Registrar of Vital Statistics, Room 613, City Hall, Buffalo, N.Y. 14202. YONKERS: Yonkers City Department of Public Health, Bureau of Vital Statistics, Yonkers, N.Y. 10701.

NORTH CAROLINA. Office of Vital Statistics, State Board of Health, P.O. Box 2091, Raleigh, N.C. 27602. Births 1913 +, deaths 1906+, marriages 1962+. Marriage records are in custody of Register of Deeds in each county. Marriage bonds from 1760 to 1968 have been published.

NORTH DAKOTA. Division of Vital Statistics, State Department of Health, 17th Floor, State Capitol, Bismarck, N. Dak. 58501. Births and deaths 1893+, marriages July 1925+. Earlier marriage records in custody of County Judge in each county.

OHIO. Division of Vital Statistics, State Department of Health, 65 S. Front Street, G-20 State Department Building, Columbus, Ohio 43215. Births and deaths 1908+, marriages 1949+. For records before those dates, write to Probate Court in county where event occurred. CLEVELAND records: births and deaths 1878+, marriages 1880 +, Cleveland City Health Department, Bureau of Vital Statistics, Room 18, City Hall, Cleveland, Ohio 44114. For marriages before 1880, write Probate Court, 1230 Ontario Street, Cleveland, Ohio 44113.

OKLAHOMA. Division of Statistics, State Department of Health, 3400 N. Eastern Avenue, Oklahoma City, Okla. 73105. Births and deaths 1908+. Marriage records are filed at the Court House in each county.

OREGON. Vital Statistics Section, State Board of Health, P.O. Box 231, Portland, Oreg. 97207. Births and deaths 1903+, marriages 1907+. Marriage records 1845+ are in custody of County Clerk of each county.

PENNSYLVANIA. Division of Vital Statistics, State Department of Health, P.O. Box 90, Harrisburg, Pa. 17120. Births and deaths 1906+. Records from 1852 to 1859 are in custody of Register of Wills in each county. Marriages before 1790 are published in Vol. 2 of Pennsylvania Archives, Series 2. PITTSBURGH records from 1870 to 1905: Allegheny County Health Department, Division of Vital Statistics, Room 637, City County Building, Pittsburgh, Pa. 15219. Records after 1905 are in Harrisburg. PHILADELPHIA records from 1860 to 1915: Vital Statistics, Philadelphia Department of Public Health, City Hall Annex, Philadelphia, Pa. 19107.

PUERTO RICO. See Chapter 4: Problem People and How to Find Them.

RHODE ISLAND. Division of Vital Statistics, State Department of Health, Room 351, State Office Building, 101 Smith St., Providence, R.I. 02903. Births, deaths, marriages: 1853+. For records before that date, write to Town Clerk in town where event occurred. Records from 1636 have been published and arranged alphabetically by town and event in the James N. Arnold *Collection of Rhode Island Vital Records.*

SOUTH CAROLINA. Bureau of Vital Statistics, State Board of Health, J. Marion Sims Building, Columbia, S. C. 29201. Births and deaths 1915+, marriages July 1950+. There are few records before the Civil War period. CHARLESTON records: births 1877+, deaths 1821+, Charleston County Health Department.

SOUTH DAKOTA. Division of Public Health Statistics, State Department of Health, Pierre, S. Dak. 57501. Births, deaths, marriages: 1906+. Marriage records before that date are in custody of Clerk of the Circuit Court at county seat.

TENNESSEE. Division of Vital Records, State Department of Public Health, Cordell Hull Building, Nashville, Tenn. 37219. Births and deaths 1914+. At the same address are birth records for Nashville 1881+, Knoxville 1881+, Chattanooga 1882+; and death records for Nashville 1872 +, Knoxville 1887+, Chattanooga 1872+. Marriage records before 1945 are in custody of County Clerk in each county.

TEXAS. Bureau of Vital Statistics, State Department of Health, 410 E. 5th Street, Austin, Tex. 78701. Births and deaths 1903+. Marriages before 1966 are in custody of County Clerk of county where license was issued. SAN ANTONIO records: births 1897+, deaths 1873+, San Antonio Metropolitan Health District, 131 W. Nueva Street, San Antonio, Tex. 78204.

UTAH. Division of Vital Statistics, State Department of Health, 44 Medical Drive, Salt Lake City, Utah 84113. Births and deaths 1905+, marriages 1954+. Records preceding those dates are kept in most counties at city and county health offices.

VERMONT. Vital Records Department, Secretary of State, State House, Montpelier, Vt. 05602. Birth and death records are in custody of Town or City Clerk where event occurred. Births 1760+, deaths 1857+, marriages 1780+.

VIRGIN ISLANDS. V.I. Department of Health, Bureau of Vital Records, Charlotte Amalie, St. Thomas, V.I. 00802. Births and deaths 1906+, marriages 1954+. Clerk of the District Court at St. Thomas has marriage records.

VIRGINIA. Bureau of Vital Records and Statistics, State Department of Health, James Madison Building, P.O. Box 1000, Richmond, Va. 23208. Births and deaths 1912+, marriages 1853+. There are also some birth and death records for 1853 to 1896. The County Clerk in each county has marriage records before 1853. Some cities had vital records before the state: Roanoke 1891+, Norfolk 1892+, Newport News 1896+, Portsmouth 1900+, Richmond 1900+, Lynchburg 1910+, Petersburg 1900+, and Elizabeth City County 1900+.

WASHINGTON. Bureau of Vital Statistics, State Department of Health, Public Health Building, Olympia, Wash. 98501. Births and deaths July 1907+, marriages 1968+. Marriage records before that date are in custody of County Auditor in each county, as well as other earlier records. SPOKANE records 1891+: Spokane City Health Department, Vital Statistics, Room 551, City Hall, Spokane, Wash. 99201. TACOMA records: births and deaths 1887+, marriages 1861+, Tacoma-Pierce County Health Department, Room 654, County-City Building, Tacoma, Wash. 98402.

WEST VIRGINIA. Division of Vital Statistics, State Department of Health, State Office Building No. 3, Charleston, W. Va. 25305. Births and deaths 1917+, marriages 1921+. Some records are in custody of County Clerk in each county.

WISCONSIN. Bureau of Health Statistics, Wisconsin Division of Health, P.O. Box 309, Madison, Wis. 53701. Births and deaths 1876+, marriages 1840+. Some records go back to 1814. Marriage records are in custody of County Clerk and of Recorder of Deeds in some counties.

WYOMING. Division of Vital Statistics, State Department of Health, State Office Building, Cheyenne, Wyo. 82001. Births and deaths 1909+, marriages 1914+. Earlier marriage records are in custody of County Clerk of each county.

Bibliography

This book only skims the surface of a fascinating, full-of-surprises hobby. If you want to learn more ways to uncover genealogical mysteries, you may wish to read some of these books which delve into the subject more deeply.

American Genealogical Research Institute Staff, *How to Trace Your Family Tree.* Doubleday & Company, Inc., Dolphin Books, 1975.

Bidlack, Russell E., *First Steps in Climbing the Family Tree,* 2d ed. Detroit Society for Genealogical Research, c/o Burton Historical Collection, Detroit Public Library, Detroit, Mich. 48202, 1960.

Colket, Meredith B., and Bridgers, Frank E., *Guide to Genealogical Records in the National Archives.* Superintendent of Documents, U.S. Government Printing Office, Washington, D.C. 20402, 1964.

Criswell, Howard Donald, *Find Your Ancestor.* P.O. Box 6286, Washington, D.C. 20015, 1970.

Daughters of the American Revolution, National Society, *Is That Lineage Right?* Corresponding Secretary, N.S.D.A.R., 1776 D Street, N.W., Washington, D.C. 20006, 1965.

Doane, Gilbert H., *Searching for Your Ancestors: The How and Why of Genealogy,* 4th ed. University of Minnesota Press, 1973.

Everton, George B., *The How Book for Genealogists.* The Everton Publishers, Logan, Utah, 1973.

Everton, George B., and Rasmuson, Gunnar, *The Handy Book for Genealogists.* The Everton Publishers, 1967.

Greenwood, Val D., *The Researcher's Guide to American Genealogy.* Genealogical Publishing Company, 1973.

Groene, Bertram H., *Tracing Your Civil War Ancestor.* John F. Blair Publisher, Winston-Salem, N.C., 1973.

Jacobus, Donald Lines, *Genealogy as a Pastime and Profession.* Genealogical Publishing Company, 1968.

Jones, Vincent L.; Eakle, Arlene H.; and Christensen, Mildred H., *Family History for Fun and Profit.* Publishers Press, Salt Lake City, Utah, 1972.

Kirkham, E. Kay, *Simplified Genealogy for Americans.* Deseret Book Company, Salt Lake City, Utah, 1968.

Pine, Leslie G., *American Origins.* Doubleday & Company, Inc., 1960.

Rubincam, Milton (ed.), *Genealogical Research Methods and Sources.* American Society of Genealogists, Washington, D.C., 1960.

Stevenson, Noel C., *Search and Research.* Deseret Book Company, Salt Lake City, Utah, 1957.

Stryker-Rodda, Kenn, *Genealogy.* Boy Scouts of America, New Brunswick, N.J. Pamphlet #3383.

Williams, Ethel W., *Know Your Ancestors.* Charles E. Tuttle Company, Inc., Rutland, Vt., 1965.

Wright, Norman E., *Building an American Pedigree.* University of Utah Press, 1974.

Zabriskie, George O., *Climbing Our Family Tree Systematically.* Parliament Press, Salt Lake City, Utah, 1969.

Many magazines and magazine articles will also help you learn how to hunt ancestors:

America Magazine, "What's in a Name?," March 5, 1966.

American Heritage, "Grandfathers of the Candidates," June 1964.

American History Illustrated, "In Search of the African," Alex Haley, February 1974.

Business Week, "Climbing Up and Down Your Family Tree," Sept. 30, 1972.

Family Circle, "How to Trace Your Family Tree," November 1972.

The Genealogical Helper. A magazine for genealogists, issued six times yearly. The Everton Publishers, P.O. Box 368, Logan, Utah 84321.

Harvest Years, "Let's Climb the Family Tree," March 1969; "Genealogy, the Mystery Hobby," August 1971; "Insurance Against Oblivion," February 1972.

Hobbies, "Genealogical Research, Basic Guide," September 1970; "Sleuthing for Ancestors," July 1971.

Holiday, "How to Prune the Family Tree," July 1972.

Horizon, "The Well-pruned Family Tree," Winter 1970.

The New York Times Magazine, "My Furthest Back Person," Alex Haley, July 16, 1972.

Retired Living, "Dear Cousins," March 1973.

The Saturday Evening Post, "It Wasn't Born Yesterday," July 27, 1963.

Saturday Review, "Blue Blood," October 29, 1966.

Scientific American, "People of York," January 1970.

Writer's Digest, "Freelance Job Idea, Genealogy," July 1971.

In addition to the above books and articles, there were many other resources that were helpful in putting this book together. Here they are:

The American Genealogical-Biographical Index. Godfrey Memorial Library, Middletown, Conn., from 1952 on.

Berry, Brewton, *Almost White.* The Macmillan Company, 1963.

Boston Transcript. Genealogical column, from June 6, 1896, to 1941.

Bremer, Ronald A., and Williams, Kendall H., 3 booklets: *Federal Forms, Sources and Repositories,* and *Things Interesting.* Gencor, Inc., Salt Lake City, Utah.

Calhoun, Arthur W., *Social History of the American Family*

from Colonial Times to the Present, Vols. I, II, III. Barnes & Noble, Inc., 1945.

Fink, Irene E. (ed.), *Directory of Libraries and Information Sources in the Philadelphia Area.* Philadelphia Chapter of the Special Libraries Association, 1973.

Frazier, E. Franklin, *The Negro Family in the United States.* The University of Chicago Press, 1939.

Gillon, Edmund Vincent, Jr., *Early New England Gravestone Rubbings.* Dover Publications, Inc., 1966.

Herskovits, Melville J., *The New World Negro.* Indiana University Press, 1966.

How to Search a Cemetery. Genealogical Institute, Publications Division, Salt Lake City, Utah, 1974.

Jacobus, Donald Lines, *Index to Genealogical Periodicals,* 3 vols. Genealogical Publishing Company, 1963–1969.

Katz, William Loren, *Eyewitness, The Negro in American History.* Pitman Publishing Corporation, 1969.

Klein, Barry T. (ed.), *Reference Encyclopedia of the American Indian,* 2d ed. Todd Publications, 1973.

Maisel, Albert Q., *They All Chose America.* Thomas Nelson & Sons, 1957.

Major Genealogical Record Sources of Indians of the United States. Genealogical Society, Series B, No. 2, 1968.

Munsell, Joel, and others, *American Ancestry: Giving the Name and Descent, in the Male Line, of Americans Whose Ancestors Settled in the U.S. Previous to the Declaration of Independence, A.D. 1776.* 12 vols. Genealogical Publishing Company, 1968.

The New England Historical and Genealogical Register, Vols. 1–112.

Rizzo, Luciano J., and Mondello, Salvatore, *The Italian-Americans.* Wayne Publishers, Inc., 1971.

Whiteman, Maxwell, *Black Genealogy.* Talk at Union League, Philadelphia, Pa., June 1971.

Your Research Dollar, Is It Doing the Most for You? Genealogical Institute, Salt Lake City, Utah, 1973.

In addition, the author read—and you probably will also—many family histories, county histories, compiled lists, genealogical and historical periodicals, letters, diaries, and pamphlets.

Supplies of interest to beginning and advanced family hunters can be found at many genealogical supply houses, including the following:

The Everton Publishers, P.O. Box 368, Logan, Utah 84321

Gencor, Inc., 322 Crandall Building, Salt Lake City, Utah 84101

Goodspeed's Book Shop, Inc., 18 Beacon Street, Boston, Mass. 02108

Stevenson's Genealogical Center, Provo, Utah 84601

Index

Bureau of Vital Statistics, 77, 78
Burials, African, as genealogical clues, 89
Buried families, 60–64

Caesar, Julius, 39
Calendar change, 50–53
Camera as hunting tool, 26, *49, 51*
Canada, 94, 144, 146
Card catalog, 58–59
Cemetery records, 48, *49,* 50–51, 69, 104–105, *159*
Census: of 1850, 94, 107; of 1890, 112
Census of dead people, 111–112
Census records, 16, 69, 73, 81; black families in, 96, 107; Indians in, 81. *Also see* State censuses
Chart, family group record, 24
Chart, personal, *10,* 11, 13; Indian, 79
Chart, research, 25, 55
Cherokee records, 81–82
Christening records (slaves), 93. *See also* Baptismal records
Church of Jesus Christ of the Latter-Day Saints, genealogical library of, 69–72
Church records, 16, 69, 80, 105
City archives, 104
City directories, 66
Civil War records, 140, 146–147
Coats of arms, 22
Compiled lists, 64
Confederate records, 146–147

County boundaries, changes of, 66, 109
County history books, 55, 72
Court-martial records, 142
Court records, 112
Criminal ancestors, 120, 126–127

Dates, how to write, 11
Daybooks, plantation, 92
Death notices, 96
Death records, 167–168
Decatur, Stephen, 136
Declaration of Independence, 144
Deeds, 28, 116, 163
Diaries, 28, 30–32, 102, 136–138, 151–152
Diploma, 32
Divorce records, 75, 77–78
Documentary proof, 101–118, 160–161
Drug addict ancestors, 127–128

Education (census), 109
Egle's Notes and Queries, 64
Eloping ancestors, 130
Emancipation records, 93
Epidemics, records of, 111–112
Esterhazy, Adam, 39

Family, size of, 48
Family card catalog, 58
Family crests, 22
Family group chart, 24
Family history books, 21, 58–60, 72, 160
Family-hunting as a job, 163
Family organizations, 160
Famous people, relationship to, 21, 22

186

Report cards, 28, *29*

Research chart, *25,* 55, 69

Researcher's Guide to American Genealogy, The, 68

Revolutionary War, 20, 129–130, 139, 144–146; Negroes in, 94

Runaway ancestors, 121–123

School records, *29;* Indian, 81–83

School yearbook, 28, 32

Scots immigrants, 86

Scrapbooks, 28, 32, 56

Self-addressed, stamped envelopes, 27, 68, 83

Sharing information, 158

Shattuck, Lemuel, 107

Shipping lists, 147–148

Sic, meaning of, 23

Silverware, *33,* 34

Slavery. *See* Black family history

Soundex system, 41–42, 110–111; for passenger lists, 147

Spelling mistakes, 41

State censuses, 112

State histories, 72

State records, 36

Supplies for genealogists, 183

Surnames, 39

Tape recorder, 14, 26

Tax records, 96, 99, 112, 115, 116

Titles for ancestors, 44, 48

Tombstone records, 48–*49, 51,* 102, 104–105, 158–*160*

Tory ancestors, 129–130, 144–146

Town histories, 16, 72

"Transported" ancestors, 120

Traveling ancestors, 149–154

Tribal history: Indian, 78–83; black, 88; enrollment records, 80

Undertaker's records, 104

Uneducated ancestors, 126

Veterans benefits records, 139–140, *143*

Visiting ancestral places, 161–163

Vital records, 102–107

Vital Statistics, Bureau of, 77, 78, 105–106, 167–168

Voting lists, 96

War heroes, 129–130, 134–147

Washington, George, 21, 52

Wedding rings, 36

William the Conqueror, 39

Wills, 16, 69, 81, 112, 113–115, 154; slaves mentioned in, 93–94

Words as clues, 89, 97

Writing letters, 22, 26–27, 67–68